THE
NETWORKING
GURU

Traits of Champion Networkers

Book 1 in the Series

Chris,

May you become the Networking Champion you were meant to be!

God Bless,

James Barber

James Barber

Wasteland Press

www.wastelandpress.net
Shelbyville, KY USA

The Networking Guru:
Traits of Champion Networkers
by James Barber

First Printing – January 2015
ISBN: 978-1-68111-005-9

Although this book is written in a fictive vein and most of the names are fictitious, some people named in the book are real people. All those whose actual names have been used in the book have given me permission to use their name. The purpose of using real names for some of the characters is to let you, the reader, know that people live by the principles in this book and enjoy the success that comes along with mastering these truths. On the following pages, you'll see a picture with a small biography and contact information for six of those named in the book. In my time being involved in various networking groups and meeting thousands of people in this arena, I have found these six people to be champion networkers. Each of them would love to have a conversation with you, so feel free to contact them.

Printed in the U.S.A.

0   1   2   3   4   5   6   7   8

This book is dedicated to Tony Devins

Shortly after my wife and I began a new business, she asked me if I thought it would be a good idea to attend a small business meeting at the local Costco. I assured her that it couldn't hurt. She went to the meeting, spoke with other business owners and left a few business cards. A couple of days later Tony Devins called and invited me to a networking meeting. Since I did not know one thing about networking meetings, I thought he was trying to sell me a get-rich-quick scheme.

He explained that his group gathered on a weekly basis to pass referrals to each other. I decided to attend his meeting. After I saw the dynamics of this meeting, I filled out an application to become part of his group. I have never looked back and feel that the best way to grow a business is by building a network of people around you to help achieve your goals and dreams. If it had not been for Tony, this book would never have been written. He gave me my start in this area of life, and I remain indebted to him.

Foreword

by Ivan Misner, Ph.D.,
New York Times Bestselling Author and Founder of BNI®

If you have a dream of having a highly successful business yet you don't have the financial capital to spend millions or even thousands of dollars on advertising to help you see your dream become a reality, this book is a must read.

In the beginning of a budding entrepreneur or small business owner's journey, he or she generally has more available time than money. This is possibly one of the reasons that a large number of businesses fail within the first five years and for those that make it through the first five years, many then fail before reaching ten years. It is devastating when a business fails because the failure is almost never due to laziness or loss of passion on the part of the business owner; it's more often due to lack of cash flow resulting from a shortage of consumers.

So what can business owners do to bring in a steady stream of customers, drive profits, and build a thriving business year after year? You will find the answer within these pages, and the answer lies in the development of a strategically designed, grass-roots, low-cost, yet highly effective referral marketing campaign.

One of the best ways for a small business owner to grow his or her business is by purposefully building trusted, symbiotically beneficial relationships with a diverse network of other business professionals with whom they can mutually refer business. The best part of this is that it can be approached in a systematic manner which has been proven effective time and time again for any given business in any given part of the world. You do not have to figure out how to do this by yourself and by investing the time to read this book, you are already well on your way to successfully constructing a powerful network that will foster your business growth.

In 1985, I started BNI® (Business Network International) with a handful of other local business professionals out of a need to bring in more clients for my own business— unbeknownst to me, the organization would evolve into what is now the world's largest referral marketing organization. This is a clear testament to the power of networking for business growth and I can confidently say that across different races, different places, and different cultures, we *all* speak the language of referrals.

In the beginning, my goal for BNI was to assemble a small group of business owners together on a regular basis for the purpose of passing qualified referrals to each other. As time progressed, however, business professionals from other areas who were not members of our group would visit and ask if they could start the same kind of group in their area. In a few years there were BNI chapters in several cities across the United States and now, nearly thirty years later, there are thousands of BNI chapters located in over 50 countries spanning the globe and the organization has a membership nearing 200,000. Through BNI's proven system for generating business referrals, we are truly *Changing the Way the World Does Business®*.

I believe Book 1 of *The Networking Guru* series, subtitled *Traits of Champion Networkers,* is a fantastic resource for those new to business networking as it not only charts a systematic path to building a network of business professionals around you, it also makes for a very compelling read as it is written in the form of a fictional story or parable. I predict that you will gain valuable insight into the inner workings of the networking world within these pages and you'll likely find yourself relating very closely to the situations described in this engaging story.

In the end, you will find yourself equipped with an understanding of not only how to network but also why you should want to network in a very specific way. In fact, I wouldn't be surprised if after digesting the business-changing tactics, tips, and strategies contained within this book, you find yourself wanting to purchase additional copies to give to others.

May you enjoy this book as much as I did and I wish you all the best in your networking endeavors.

The Biographies

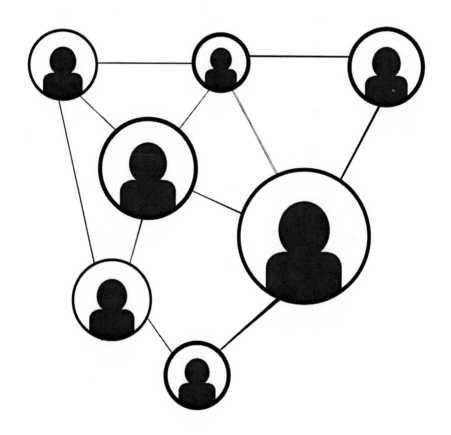

Art Kleve

With over 35 years of experience, Art Kleve is a veteran of the auto industry. After graduating from college in 1977, Art was a line supervisor with Chrysler and then moved on to be the program manager for the Mustang convertible program—the largest in the U.S. at the time. Art was then hired to oversee the Oldsmobile convertible program, supervising all areas from research and development through production. His vast experience includes plant management at Volvo Truck engine and axle and then as the Quality Division Manager. In 2003, Art became owner and operator of Nobody's Auto and Repair, where he established a solid reputation in the Lawrenceville, Loganville, Grayson, Snellville, Duluth and Suwanee communities. Nobody's continues to be a family-owned business and strives to be your "One-Stop Honest Auto Repair Shop" where integrity and outstanding repair service are our trademarks.

Contact Information:
Website: www.nobodysautorepair.com
Phone: 770-277-6320

David Gray Alexander

David's vision is to create an environment where his clients can embrace a lifestyle of high achievement. David accomplishes this through being the CNO (Chief Networking Officer) of High Achievers Training.

David conveys his passion for teaching people how to create success and live a lifestyle of achievement with a strong emphasis on referral marketing in his #1 best selling book: *Networking Like a Pro: Turning Contacts into Connections*, co-authored with Dr. Ivan Misner and Brian Hilliard. He's also a featured author of *Roadmap to Success*, along with Ken Blanchard and Stephen Covey, and *Steeping Stones to Success* with Jack Canfield.

David is also the Executive Director of BNI and runs one of the largest BNI regions in the world. David and his company have won numerous awards with BNI and are currently in the Hall of Fame and Platinum Club. BNI is the world's leading business referral organization.

David is a graduate of Western Carolina University. He currently resides with his wife, Kimberly, their two children, Christian and Peyton, and two golden retrievers in Marietta, Georgia.

Contact Information:
E-mail: david@referrals4life.com
Website: www.BNIsoutheast.com and
www.HighAchievers.com
Phone: 678.888.0200

David Lawler

David Lawler is a general practice attorney in the northern Atlanta, Georgia suburbs. While he handles many areas of law, his focus is on real estate transactions and domestic/family law. (He's one of the few happily married divorce attorneys you'll ever meet.)

Contact Information:
Law Offices of David M. Lawler, Inc.
www.dlawler.com

Gina Herald

Gina Herald is a coach, trainer, speaker and the owner of Personal Success Partners, a personal and professional development company. They work with companies to develop the next generation of leaders, put customer service culture in place, improve internal and external communication and increase sales.

Gina has over 20 years of leadership experience across a broad spectrum of industries. She has served on non-profit boards and has helped start several small businesses. She attributes her success to many things including a strong and resilient faith, the courage to admit she needs help, the strength to ask for it and the network of incredible people with whom she has had the good fortune to be associated.

Contact Information:
www.personalsuccesspartners.com and
www.linkedin.com/in/ginaherald

Derek Sutton

Derek worked in Corporate America for 20+ years. He is a certified trainer with High Achievers Training. He is also a BNI Director overseeing 10 BNI chapters in the Atlanta area. He currently co-owns Pop-N-Go Repair Pros, which repairs cracked screens on smart phones and I-pads.

He has been married for 18 years, and he and his wife have three children.

Keys to success: Always put God first; listen to others and treat them how you want to be treated; and never compromise your morals.

Contact Information:
Pop-N-Go Repair Pros
Office: 404-376-0048
www.popngorepair.com
E-mail: dlsutton@popngorepair.com

Cathy Barbieri

Cathy Barbieri has a degree in mass communications from Middle Tennessee State. Cathy has consistently been involved in sales and marketing. She became involved as a member of BNI in 1995. A year after joining BNI she was selected to assist chapter members as a BNI Director. Cathy transforms the way sales teams utilize networking to build strategic referral relationships.

She and her husband, Mike, own Carpet DryClean of Atlanta, an Organic carpet cleaning company. Additionally, she works with BNI Southeast, which has chapters in Georgia and North Carolina. She serves as Director of Referral Development.

Contact Information:
E-mail: cathy@bnisoutheast.com

THE
NETWORKING
GURU

Traits of Champion Networkers

Book 1 in the Series

TABLE OF CONTENTS

CHAPTER 1

Introduction

"I just need to quit!" voiced Clark.

Charlene lovingly chimed in with, "I know our financial situation stinks. Paying the bills takes every dime we can scrape together. Since we decided to start A+ Pest Control, our life has changed somewhat, and I hate to see you notably frustrated. Let's give it six more months. If things do not look better, we can shut down the business, and you can work for another company."

"I am extremely thankful that you are my wife. Your encouragement means the world to me; however, I didn't know it would be this difficult to build a profitable business. Although my energy has always been high, this endeavor is sapping my strength."

"I understand," replied Charlene. "I just had an excellent thought. Give your friend Mike a call. As you know, he and his brothers had a medical supply business that they built from nothing. He may have some suggestions."

"Thanks for the tip. I will call him. Again, I love you more than words can describe, and I'm thankful you are my wife."

Clark had worked in the pest control industry for years and had learned the business from the ground up. His peers in the industry considered Clark an expert in treating homes and commercial structures for pests and termites. As his reputation for excellence and honesty grew, many friends encouraged him to start his own business. After a tremendous amount of planning and prayer, Clark and Charlene committed to building the best pest control business in Georgia.

Though Clark knew the pest control industry and had a dream of establishing a valuable pest control business, he didn't understand all of the dynamics that it takes to produce and operate a successful business. Following in the path of many other business owners, he started with his dream and the money that he could muster. He didn't understand that just because you are good at an occupation doesn't mean that customers will knock down your doors to do business with you.

Obtaining the right licenses, equipment and insurance for his new pest control business took many months and a sizable investment. He also purchased a website, multiple yellow page ads and marketing materials, like door hangers and flyers. He told friends and family that his company was fully operational and ready for business. After months of pounding the pavement, only a few people had signed up for services. As the weeks passed, they would get an occasional call from the website or a door hanger but nothing from the other advertising.

After a hot and irritating day of passing out flyers with no results, he called his friend Mike to discuss his options. A few days prior, his wife had advised him to call Mike for some suggestions since he had previously owned a business.

"Mike, I am discouraged. As you know, we started our pest control company six months ago; however, we are floundering. We have tried several avenues to gain customers, but we have failed. I think we need to close up shop and work for another company."

"You can't quit, Clark. You love what you do, and you're the best. My brothers and I owned a business in New York. We began our business just like you did. We didn't have any customers, and we had to start from the beginning. I feel your pain because I have been there."

"Thanks for the sympathy, Mike. Since you have been through this before, do you have any words of wisdom that you can impart?"

"I could give you a few pointers, but why don't you try something different. I've heard of a man that everyone calls the networking guru. They say he knows everyone and helps struggling, small business owners get their businesses on the right track."

"Mike, I appreciate the encouragement, and I'm so glad that you know someone who may be able to help. Do you know how much he charges or how to reach him? We sure do need the help, but we've put all of our available funds into the business."

"Clark, the local Chamber of Commerce has a meeting every Friday at 9:00 a.m., and I've heard that he's usually there," replied Mike. "I know you're dismayed right now, but he might be able to help you. I don't know him personally; but I will go with you to the meeting just to see what he looks like. I probably will only stay long enough to meet him and then leave."

"Wonderful! I'll meet you Friday."

On Friday when Clark and Mike arrived at the Chamber of Commerce building, they walked inside, and Clark asked one of the staff members, "Who is in charge of the 9:00 a.m. program?"

The staff member replied, "Kim Jones. While you fill out the information on the sign-in sheet, I'll find her and introduce you."

As soon as Clark and Mike had completed the paperwork, a young lady with a rich smile walked over to the check-in table.

"Kim, I'd like to introduce you to Clark Bowman and Mike Vernola. Clark owns a new pest control company."

"Welcome, Clark and Mike. We are delighted to have you today," said Kim. "Did someone invite you or did you find us on the Internet?"

"Mike told me about the meeting," replied Clark. "He met me here today so we could attend the meeting together."

"Has anyone explained the order of our meeting today?" asked Kim.

Clark shook his head and answered, "No."

"I'll go over it with you. For the first 10 minutes, we have open networking when people meet and greet each other. Next, we have a two-minute sponsor who tells us about their business. After that, a Chamber member gives a 7-minute presentation about their business. This person must attend the meetings regularly and have been a member for at least three months. At the conclusion of this portion of the meeting, everyone stands and has 30 seconds to promote their business. We end with special announcements and give away door prizes that members bring. Everyone then has the opportunity to spend time talking with others before leaving."

"Thanks, Kim. I appreciate all of this information, but I have a question. Mike wanted me to talk with a man who comes to this meeting; some people call him the networking guru. Do you know him?"

"Yes, that would be Timothy Carter," answered Kim. "He owns Business Champions and knows everybody. I'll introduce you to him."

They walked through the crowded room.

"Tim, I want to introduce you to Clark Bowman and his friend, Mike. This is their first time at a meeting, and Clark owns a new pest control business."

"What a pleasure to meet you," confirmed Timothy with a friendly smile. "Has anyone explained how the meeting works?"

Kim gave them a wave and made her way back through the crowded room.

"Yes, Kim graciously explained the process," replied Clark.

"Great! Come with me, and I'll introduce you to a few of the members."

As they walked away, Clark commented that Kim was very nice and extremely helpful.

"I agree," responded Timothy. "Even though she works for the Chamber, it's more than a job for her. She has a genuine concern for the members, and she wants to see the members' businesses grow."

"Mr. Carter, how do you want me to address you?" asked Clark.

"Whatever makes you comfortable," he answered. "You can call me whatever you like; just don't call me late for supper. Most of my friends call me Tim."

"Ok. I'll call you Tim because I want to be one of your friends," replied Clark.

During the open networking portion of the meeting, Tim introduced Clark to a Goodwill Ambassador for the Chamber of Commerce, a REALTOR® named Johnny Holliman. Then Clark met another Realtor named Betty McCaleb, a plumber named John Bell, and a general contractor named Rob Bailey.

Even though Kim had already gone over the meeting agenda, Tim discussed the schedule of events again.

Mike explained to Tim and Clark that he needed to leave. He said his goodbyes to both before he left.

"Clark, when it comes time for people to introduce themselves, some members will have a practiced speech and others will not. Some will be humorous; some use current events to advertise their business; some have the same speech every time; and others change from time to time. One member occasionally sings his presentation, and another man uses poetry. How people choose to market themselves varies.

"Since this is your first time, just keep it simple. State your name, your company name, you are in the termite and pest control industry, and end with your name and company name. The microphone is directional, so hold it approximately two inches from your mouth and speak clearly into it. Even though this is your first time, you want people to understand your message."

"Thanks, Tim," answered Clark. "I'll do my best."

At the meeting, there were 15 first-time guests and a total of 95 people. Forty of the members had been active in the

Chamber for at least five years. Ann Ladeaux facilitated the meeting, and Pat Bonice was the co-facilitator. A Chamber staff member, Meagan Lundquist, greeted everyone, recognized the volunteer Ambassadors, asked everyone to silence their cell phones and turned the remainder of the meeting over to Ann.

Ann introduced the two-minute sponsor, Cakes with a Plan. The owner discussed making cakes for any occasion and for any theme. She described how she was a master at making cakes and that she was looking to meet event planners. Tim wrote a note to Clark explaining that her cakes were indeed excellent, and she had baked many cakes for him.

After the two-minute sponsor, Ann explained that there would be a seven-minute presenter, and later everyone would have 30 seconds to introduce his or her business. Pat gave instructions for passing a lead to another attendee.

"When we finish with the infomercials," Ann stated, "we'll ask how many leads were passed in the past week, make some special announcements, give away door prizes and then we'll finish with some more open networking.

"Now I'd like to introduce our seven-minute presenter," announced Ann. "He and his wife own Make it Live Website Construction Company. They have been in business for over 15 years and have won numerous awards. Before deciding to launch their company, both husband and wife worked in corporate America for several years. By crafting a creative website that's within budget, they help entrepreneurs grow by giving them extensive exposure in cyberspace. They can work with a budget of $300 to $100,000. Without further ado, put your hands together and help make welcome Dave and Sharon Green."

The couple gave an enthusiastic presentation about website design.

When they finished, Ann stated, "Now that we know more about what Dave and Sharon do, let's find them some prospects who can use their services."

After Dave and Sharon returned to their seats, Ann announced, "It's now time for our infomercials. Everyone will have 30 seconds to promote his or her business. Start with your name and company name, tell us what you do, and end with your name and company name. If during this time someone has a product or a service that interests you, fill out the sheet of paper on your table designated for leads. We will give it to that individual at the end of the meeting. If two or more people are from the same company, then one person speaks and introduces the other members of your team. Once the beeper sounds, pass the microphone to the next member. One last thing, the microphone is directional so hold it approximately 2 inches from your mouth so that everyone will be able to hear you."

The infomercials ranged from serious to funny. Most long-standing members were well-spoken and well-prepared, while others, especially the guests, appeared somewhat nervous.

"Everyone, pass your lead sheets to the middle. Ambassadors, give them to the appropriate person. Thank you, my fellow ambassadors," Ann affirmed.

Kim read some special announcements that dealt with charities. When the leads that had been passed in the previous week were counted, there were 76.

Ann stated, "Johnny, our resident MC, will announce the door prizes and draw for the winners."

"This is the part of the meeting where enthusiasm is encouraged, and we would like the giver and the receiver of the door prize to stand when we call your name," Johnny declared.

The 7-minute presenter, Dave Green, who always brings a jar of jelly beans for his door prize, told Johnny that today they were giving away jelly bean number five million. Several members were excited because they had a chance to win the five millionth jelly bean.

Once the 12 door prizes were passed out, Ann confirmed, "We have 95 people in attendance and passed 76 leads.

Everyone have a good weekend, and we'll see you next week."

Clark asked Tim, "Is the meeting always this much fun to attend? It seemed like everyone was happy to be here and engaged in the process. I thoroughly enjoyed myself and would like to return."

Tim encouraged Clark to do so and asked if he would like to have lunch.

"That would be wonderful."

"What kind of food do you like?" asked Tim.

"Just about anything works for me," replied Clark.

"A friend of mine, D.P. Patel, owns the Philly Connection, so let's go there."

"That works for me."

When they arrived at the Philly Connection, Tim greeted the owner heartily with, "Hello, D. P. Good to see you again. I'll have the usual and whatever my friend wants."

Clark finally decided on a Philly with mushrooms and jalapeño peppers. Tim paid for both of their meals. While they waited for their food, Tim asked Clark why he had come to the Chamber of Commerce meeting.

"I actually came to see you. Mike told me that you are considered to be the networking guru and that you might be able to help me."

After their food arrived, they continued their conversation.

Tim asked, "How may I help you?"

Clark replied, "Do you have enough time for me to tell you my story?"

"We have the rest of the afternoon if we need it."

"Fantastic!" voiced Clark. "I've worked in the termite and pest control industry for 13 years. Approximately two years ago, my wife and I decided to start our own business. We went through a lengthy process for launching our new company. We have been in business for six months, but we are extremely frustrated.

"When I worked for other companies, I became extremely proficient in the field. I learned to control termites and other pests as efficiently as the leading experts in the Country. Since my skill set and knowledge ranked high in the industry, I thought that customers would come running to do business with us. This has not happened.

"We have tried many different things such as a website, phone book advertising, passing out door hangers and "word of mouth" to family and friends. We have a few customers, but not nearly as many as we thought we would have by now. I just don't know what to do. We have considered closing down the business and working for another company. Do you have any suggestions about how we can grow our customer base?"

"I do, and I will be glad to help you. You have to agree, however, to some conditions," expressed Tim. "Your story is a mirror image of many others."

"What kind of conditions?"

"First and foremost, you must apply yourself to everything you learn. The process will take one week. The first day I'll teach you about growing your business through building a network around you.

"Every day for seven consecutive days, you'll learn about networking from a different expert, including spending your first day with me covering some basics. Each person will spend about two hours with you. Every day you'll learn about a specific networking topic. There will possibly be some overlap because each person that you will be introduced to may say some of the same things that one or more of the others have said, but they will cover a specific topic in detail. Commonalities among the various components of networking will be evident by the time you finish the program.

"The second crucial condition is you review what you are taught on a daily basis. If one of the experts gives you an exercise to practice, you must practice until you become proficient at that particular portion of networking.

"The third condition is that once you have mastered the principles of networking, you must help other business owners learn the art of networking."

"Ok, Tim, I agree to all of the conditions. I have one additional question. How much money will this cost me? I don't mind paying to receive the help, but I don't want to over extend myself."

"The cost will be affordable, but we'll discuss that when you finish with the program."

"I hope you are correct about the affordability because I really do not want to shell out more money than what I have."

They stopped their conversation until they had finished eating their delicious Philly sandwiches.

"Clark, have you heard of the restaurant called, Curt's? It's approximately 20 miles north of here."

"Yes. Isn't it off of Exit 16?"

"That's correct."

"A few years ago, I was working in that area, and a friend suggested eating breakfast there. I remember they had outstanding biscuits," stated Clark.

"Let's meet at Curt's in the morning at 8 a.m. We'll eat breakfast, and then we'll begin."

CHAPTER 2

The System

On Saturday morning at 8 a.m., Clark and Tim met for breakfast at Curt's. Tim ordered eggs over medium, hash browns, bacon and a buttermilk, cathead biscuit. Clark ordered a fried egg, ham and cheese breakfast sandwich. After they ordered breakfast, they got down to it.

"Tim, do you care if I record our conversation so I can make sure I don't miss anything?"

"That's fine, Clark."

"What you will learn over the next few days applies to someone like you, a business owner, but the principles contained in this training program also apply for sales professionals. Many sales professionals are taught to make cold calls, or to knock on doors for the purpose of talking to people whom they don't know. They are taught that if they talk to enough people they will find someone who will purchase their products and/or services. Although medical science does not have a cure for the common cold, what you will learn is a system to cure the common cold.

"Some people have a beehive of activity without any honey. When I was a young man, an elderly man said to me one day, 'Son, you need to learn to work smarter and not harder.'"

"Tim, I remember my dad saying that."

"Have you ever heard the saying that it takes a man and a woman to produce children, but it takes a village to raise them?"

Clark nodded.

Tim continued, "Every person is the sum total of what has been deposited in their life. Some of the people who make contributions to our lives include, but are not limited to, parents, grandparents, aunts, uncles, cousins, teachers, religious leaders and mentors.

"When it comes to growing a business, people can do what you did by starting with a dream, purchasing some advertising and other marketing materials and promoting their business by themselves, or they can become involved in organizations that will partner with them to promote their business.

"Let me put it to you like this. If a car broke down in the street and needed to be moved to the side of the street so that other traffic could pass, a man could try to push the car and steer it by himself. That would be difficult. If another man joins him, it becomes a little bit easier, but it is still somewhat difficult. On the other hand, if 10 or 12 people join in the push, then moving the car goes much smoother.

"Clark, does this concept register with you?"

"It does, and that is exactly what I have tried to do. I have been trying to push and steer the car by myself; furthermore, I feel like I've been pushing the car up the side of Mount Everest. With limited funds, I just did not know what to do."

"Clark, the most cost effective way for a business owner to grow his or her business is by building a network of other business professionals around them. The terminology that many people use for this avenue simply goes by the name of networking. Various ideas and concepts exist about networking, but over the next few days, you'll learn from specialists in this field the most effective traits to have in order to maximize the results from your networking efforts."

"Networking has been around for thousands of years, and in certain cultures, it is stronger than in others. One purpose for having a network around you is to help you achieve your goals, ambitions and dreams. Many people in our lives can support us in that endeavor."

Tim sipped his coffee.

"In the last 30 years or so, there have been some fantastic leaders in business networking. I encourage you to read books written by Dr. Ivan Misner, founder of BNI, Brian Tracy, Bob Burg, Michael Gerber and Don Morgan. They have masterfully written books on networking or topics related to networking."

"I sure will."

"Let's discuss a few things about networking that are vital to business success. As Michael Gerber of the famous *E-Myth* book says, 'With all things being equal, people will generally do business with people that they know, like and trust.' What does that mean to you? "

"In the pest control industry, there are at least 100 companies in the metro area. Some companies are large and have many employees. Some are medium-sized, and others are like your company which operates with one or two employees.

"Ten percent of the people will only do business with a large company, and ten percent will never do business with a large company. Eighty percent of people don't have a preference on the size of the company. The majority of people will do business with the person that earns their trust, even if the cost is a little more. Does that make sense?" concluded Tim.

Clark thought about it for a minute. His paralyzing discouragement had caused him to think that he couldn't compete with the big guys. He nodded his head slowly. "Yes. Now I understand what you mean."

"Let's break down the word networking. This compound word is comprised of two smaller words. The first word is *net*. A net is used primarily for capturing an intended target. People use nets for capturing butterflies, and they also use nets to catch fish.

"All over the World people fish by casting nets, keeping what they need and throwing back the rest. If you threw a net into a lake in Georgia, you might catch some combination of bass, brim, catfish and carp. You might like bass the best, but you can eat everything except the carp. They are good for eating algae in the lake, but are not edible.

"Imagine someone hauling in a net and sorting through the fish. He picks up a bass by placing his thumb in the mouth of the bass, holding it by the lower lip and then tosses it into a basket to keep. Without looking closely, he reaches to pick up the next fish the same way, but it's a barracuda that bites off his thumb.

"When you go to a business event to meet people, you are casting a net. Like in fishing, when you are networking, you have to sort through the relationships and carefully separate the good from the bad. If business professionals always want to know what you can do for them and they never ask what they can do to help you, then they are like that barracuda. They will destroy you and never think twice about it."

Tim paused a moment while the waitress refilled his coffee cup.

"Clark, have you ever been around someone who seems to suck the life out of you?"

"Yes," answered Clark thoughtfully. "I know a few people like that. They always have their hand out for money or want something, but they never give to others."

"An old saying exists that says, 'Give a man a fish, feed him for a day, but teach him to fish and you feed him for a lifetime,'" voiced Tim.

"I've heard that saying before," stated Clark.

"Tim, when I worked for one company, I had a customer that every time I went to her house, she had a bad day. I believe if someone gave her one million dollars, she would find something about which to complain."

"Think about other people who, every time you see them, add value to your life. You look forward to being around them."

"Yes," replied Clark. "I have people that add joy to my life. Being near them infuses me with life."

"That's right, Clark. When you cast out the net of life, you want to keep these people around you. They will be beneficial for you, and you will be beneficial for them. Although networking barracudas and piranhas will make their way into your net, make sure to carefully discard them or they will destroy you."

Tim drank some coffee.

"The second word is *working*," continued Tim. "Some people think networking requires no effort, other than attending a meeting. Those people receive little benefit. Those who are willing to work at throwing out the net will surround themselves with people who can help feed them and their family. It's not good enough to just show up."

Clark nodded his head acknowledging his understanding.

"There are three main types of networking groups. Champion networkers will belong to all three. When a person belongs to more than three groups, it doesn't allow him or her enough time to work on additional aspects of his or her business. Some people will belong to five or more networking groups. Their thought process is the more networking groups I join the merrier.

"A lady that I know belonged to approximately 10 different networking groups. One day, she attended the Chamber meeting that we went to yesterday. She quickly ascertained who the top networkers were. I happened to be out of town, but someone told her that she needed to call me. Even though I had talked with her several times over a 2-year period, she did not know me. She called me and introduced herself. After I explained that I had known her for at least two years and had shaken hands with her at least 20 times, she apologized for not remembering me.

"These types of people are generally hunters. Networking is more about farming than hunting. A hunter goes for the kill, and their focus remains on the kill. A hunter has the perception that we need to make this real quick. I can't take too much time with another networker because I must move to the next victim.

"You will run across hunters in networking. They belong to several groups, and they do not have any loyalty to anyone except themselves. They are in the same category as the barracuda and the piranha.

"You will also encounter the farmer in networking. A farmer has to prepare the soil, plant the seeds, pull the weeds, water the seeds and pick the crop at harvest time. This person realizes just as it takes time to cultivate a bountiful garden, it also takes time to cultivate bountiful relationships with those in his or her network. The hunt takes very little time, but growing a crop takes quite a bit of time. You want to be a networking farmer."

"That's a good example. I like that," Clark exclaimed.

"Networking group number one is a service-based organization like the Kiwanis, Rotary or Lions Clubs. With this type of networking group, you should not look for business but look to serve the community in which you live. Because people will have the opportunity to spend time with you, they will learn to like and trust you. They will, in turn, use your company and even refer you to their family, friends and coworkers.

"Networking group number two is an open or casual contact networking group. Examples of this type of group are the Chamber of Commerce and business associations for cities such as the Dacula Business Association and the Buford Business Alliance. Open networking groups derive their classification from the fact that they are open to any business that wants to join. This type of group will give you exposure to many businesses and business owners. At a networking meeting, there may be five real estate agents, ten insurance agents and seven website designers. Many of these groups have weekly or monthly networking meetings. Some groups also have monthly or quarterly evening gatherings which allow for socializing with other business professionals in a relaxed atmosphere.

"Networking group number three is a closed networking group where only one company represents one industry. For example, a chapter would allow only one pest control company, one property and casualty insurance agent, one financial advisor, and one website designer, etc. Some examples of closed groups are BNI, North Georgia Business Connection, Networking Works and the Metro Networking Council. BNI is an international organization with chapters worldwide, but most groups of this type are local. Some people will prefer one closed group over another based solely upon the accountability standards. Some groups have a high level of accountability, but others do not.

"All of these groups have their place, and a small business owner should belong to all three types of groups. The closed networking group will yield the fastest return on investment, and the other two types of networking groups will be a little bit slower in producing results. A business owner must understand this because if he or she expects the same results in the same time frame he or she will be sorely disappointed. The results from the combination of all three can be amazing.

"Clark, do you have any questions so far?"

"Not at this time."

Tim continued, "Another type of networking group is a business association. People in the same field come together for education or to buy group benefits such as business insurance. I looked up a couple of organizations that would be industry-specific to you, and they are Certified Pest Control Operators and Georgia Pest Control Association. As you develop relationships with other members, you can give referrals to people needing pest control outside of your service area. You can also receive referrals from those who do not work in your area. Even if you only give and receive five referrals per year, everyone still benefits."

Tim paused again to let the waitress know he didn't need any more coffee.

"One common mistake that people make when they begin their networking journey is thinking that they must sell their product or service that day. At any networking event, if you asked the entire audience, 'How many people are here to buy something?' most of them would not raise their hands. If you asked, 'How many people are here to sell something?' many people would raise their hands. The champion networker would never raise his or her hand to the last question because he or she recognizes that networking is not about selling at that time.

"At many networking functions, a visitor will approach someone that they do not know, shove a business card in a member's face, and tell the member how he or she can save him or her money on insurance or that he or she can make him or her number one on Google. Approaching people in this manner tends to aggravate them.

"Remember an important point that I stated earlier, Michael Gerber in his *E-Myth* book says, 'With all things being equal, people will generally do business with people that they know, like and trust.' When a guest at a networking meeting becomes pushy or overbearing, then the opposite of what they want happens."

"Clark, do you have any questions?"

"Yes," answered Clark. "What does it cost to join the different networking groups?"

"A service group can cost a couple hundred bucks or so per year. A Chamber of Commerce can cost $200-$1000 per year, depending on the size of the city or metro area. A city business association may cost as little as $100 per year. A closed networking group will usually cost $300 to $1500 per year.

"Certain Chambers have a higher level of membership that may cost $3000 to $10,000 per year. Some other groups with higher levels can cost as much as $15,000 per year. These last two groups predominantly serve the business-to-business community. They are designed for CEO's and high-level executives of larger corporations."

"Tim, what would be the best use of my funds if I can only join one or two?" asked Clark.

"The closed networking group like BNI will usually give you the best return on investment. A person can build those relationships quicker in the closed networking group. The second group to join would be an open networking group.

"When a person has a specialized niche, then an open networking group can produce results for them as fast as a closed group. An example of a specialized niche would be an appliance repair company; however, the open networking group will usually have several insurance agents, bankers and realtors.

"Companies often have systems in place that facilitate employees becoming successful. A system will allow ordinary people to achieve extraordinary results predictably. Each part, component or aspect of networking is a system within itself. Smaller systems comprise the entire networking system. When one follows the system, astounding results happen. In the days that follow, you'll be introduced to different practitioners who will teach you a different aspect of the networking system.

"Remember, you agreed to study what you have been taught on a daily basis, and if there is a practice portion, you must practice. You want to perfect the craft of networking. The system will work, but you have to follow the entire system. If someone thinks that the system is a la carte, i.e., that they can choose what they like and disregard what they do not like, the results will not be maximized. Do you have any questions about anything that we have discussed?"

"Not at this time. I know this is the first day of seven, but you have definitely given me several things to ponder. I sure do thank you for taking time out of your busy schedule to work with me."

"You're welcome. Since tomorrow is Sunday, let's meet after Church at Curt's for lunch. I should be able to be there by 1:00 p.m. I can't do anything on an empty stomach. When we finish, we'll drive to Lawrenceville. Your next instructor will teach you one of the components of networking," affirmed Tim.

"I'll see you then, and thanks again for your help," avowed Clark.

CHAPTER 3

Infomercials

The next afternoon, Tim and Clark sat at a table at Curt's.

"Did you have a good night?" questioned Clark.

"I did and thanks for asking," responded Tim. "How was your evening?"

"My wife and I spent some time with our six-year-old grandson, Ethan. He has brought a tremendous amount of joy to our life."

After they both ate their lunch consisting of roast beef, mashed potatoes, biscuits, Pepsi and banana pudding, Tim said, "We'll rendezvous with our next networking expert in Lawrenceville. You can leave your car here, and we'll take my car."

"That sounds good to me."

On the drive to Lawrenceville, Tim began to question Clark on what he had learned the previous day. Clark was able to answer all the questions that Tim asked.

"Clark, if you study what everyone teaches you and learn it well, you'll indeed become a wonderful and profitable networker."

"Thanks, Tim. That is my goal."

"The next person that you'll spend some time with is Art Kleve. He owns Nobody's Automotive which is a repair shop. His very profitable business has been built principally by networking. By nature, he is a shy person, but when you see him in his element of networking, you'd never know that."

When they arrived at Nobody's Automotive, Tim made the introductions.

"I'm going to run some errands, and I'll return in two hours," said Tim. "Art will teach you an enormous amount of information about his area of expertise. See you in a couple of hours."

As Tim left, Art motioned for Clark to have a seat.

"Tim tells me that you have your own pest control business."

"That's right," responded Clark. "I've been in the industry for 13 years, but we opened our own business six months ago. How long have you owned Nobody's Automotive?"

"We have owned it for 11 years. For over 20 years, I worked in the automotive industry for one of the big American automakers and then decided I'd like to own some type of automotive shop. At first, we considered buying a transmission shop, but my wife was totally opposed to that idea. When this shop became available, my wife foresaw that this would be an ideal business for us. The reason that we've been successful is that we try to do what is best for the customer every time.

"Almost every automobile that comes into the shop has several things that could be repaired. A customer may have 40 percent left on their front brake pads; they may have a small oil leak that does not even leak out four ounces between oil changes; or they may have 30 percent of tread left on their tires. We could tell our customers that all of these items must be repaired, but they really do not need to be repaired at this time.

"Before we bought Nobody's Automotive, my daughter went to a big name automotive repair and tire store to have her tires rotated. We bought the tires at this store because it came with a free lifetime rotation and balance. While she was having her tires rotated, they said they found several other repairs that needed to be made. The cost was going to be $979. My daughter called me crying, and said, 'Daddy, they are telling me the vehicle is not safe, and they can't allow me to leave until the repairs are made.' I told her I'd be there in a few minutes.

"When I arrived, I asked to be shown not only the list of repairs, but also the car myself. They showed me the list of repairs, one of which was front brake pads and rotors. I looked at the brake pads and they had 50 percent of the pad left and the rotors looked fine, as well. The technician said, 'When I put the micrometer on the rotors, they were not within specs for being safe.' I told him I would like to see him put the micrometer on them myself. He refused. I told the manager we didn't want any repairs performed and to finish the tire rotation, and we would leave. We never went back to that place again.

"Many of the automotive/tire places try to upsell a person when they have their tires rotated. Most of those repairs are not needed at that particular time. We never try to upsell people. We tell our customers what we find and let them make their own decision."

"Art, how did you come up with the name, Nobody's?"

"The previous owner had the name because they did all types of automotive repair, except body work. We kept the name because we still do all kinds of automotive repair, except body work. We can do any type of repair on any type of automobile.

"When we first bought the business, the previous owner had a few customers who would regularly use his shop. If we were going to keep our doors open, we could not count on the few customers that used his shop. We tried different kinds of advertising, but the best thing that we have ever done has been building a network of people around us who want to help us be successful. I'm sure Tim has told you that establishing a network is work, but if you network according to a system, the benefits outweigh the work. Tim understands this, and his business associates also understand this concept. Let's get started."

"I'm ready."

"We are going to talk about commercials today. But first, I want you to understand that at networking meetings you are not trying to sell to the members or guests who attend."

"Art, I don't want to question you, because it looks like you are successful. Tim brought me here because he believes in you, but why would we want to attend a meeting if we're not there to sell?"

"That's a terrific question. Research tells us that the average person knows 250 people. When we get together on Friday at the Chamber of Commerce, we're educating members and guests about what we do and what kind of referrals we need. In essence, we become the sales manager, and the members become our sales team. We want them to refer us to their 250 friends, relatives and associates.

"Members do get sales from other members, but those sales are a byproduct of networking. If you need insurance, a website, plumbing repairs, or any other service, why not use a trusted team member from your network. Everyone in the network must remember that they are not actively selling to each other; they are selling through each other.

"Clark, your company is probably a one-man or two-man operation, but as time goes on you'll add employees. One marvelous benefit of belonging to a networking group and having this kind of sales team in place is you don't have to fund payroll taxes for them or provide them benefits which cost you, the business owner.

"For open and closed networking groups, regardless of the name of the networking group, a person usually has the opportunity to broadcast a commercial about their business for 30 to 60 seconds. A 30-to-60 second commercial of a person's business goes by different names such as: infomercial, sales manager minute, elevator speech or weekly presentation. For the sake of discussion, I will refer to it as an infomercial.

"A prevalent amount of people do not practice their infomercials. They simply show up at the meeting and wing it. If you're a chicken, it's ok to wing it, but I don't see feathers growing on any of the people who attend networking meetings.

"Although variances exist when giving an infomercial, two main thought processes exist for champion networkers. Regardless of the process one chooses to use, there are key essentials that should be included in each infomercial every single time. Let's discuss the first thought process. Are you with me thus far?"

"I am."

Thought Process #1

Components of the Infomercial:

"A person should state their name, company name, one specific thing that they do, which is commonly called the lowest common denominator (or LCD for short), details or a story related to their LCD, a specific referral by name and company, and end with their name, company name and possibly a tagline or memory hook. We're going to talk about the reason for each of these.

"A person needs to hear your name and company name seven to ten times before they recognize it. For this reason, you should say your name and company name during your infomercial. One faction of networkers teaches you to say your name and company name at the beginning and also at the end, which is fine if you have the time. If a person has 60 seconds, then he or she can say their name and company name twice. With less than a minute, you may not have time to repeat your name and company name. The name and company name are for branding purposes.

"In the pest control industry, I'm sure you control different bugs, but focus on one bug or one particular service that you offer. That is the lowest common denominator (or LCD) that I mentioned earlier. Give one LCD, and tell a story connected to the LCD. Tim likes to say, 'If you talk about too many different things that you do, it will blow people's minds.' He also likes to say, 'It might not be much of an explosion, but it will still blow their minds.' Tell us one thing that you do. If you have several different things that you do, focus on one thing for a month.

"At our shop, we service every make and model of vehicle, and we provide all services for the vehicle, except auto body repair. When we break down our LCD's, we may talk about maintenance items for one month. Examples of these are: oil change, tune up, tire rotation, and transmission service.

"The next month we may discuss rebuilt engines and transmissions. If we try to talk about all of our capabilities at once, the group can't process so many services at one time.

"When we attend a networking meeting, we are educating our sales team. We have to keep them focused on one LCD, because we don't want to blow their minds. Tell me how this could apply to you."

Clark paused for a moment before saying thoughtfully, "I could talk about roach control one month, the next month ant control and then termite control."

"That's right," said Art. "I think you understand this part. We could say, 'If a person changes the oil in their vehicle on a regular basis, it will prolong the life of their vehicle by up to 50 percent. We just changed the oil in a Kia Sportage that has 350,000 miles on it.'"

"Wow!" Clark exclaimed.

Art paused for a minute before he continued.

"When asking for a referral, make it as specific as possible. A good referral for our business is someone who owns a fleet of vehicles. If I ask for the referral that way, then that could be anyone so the members think of no one. When asking for a referral, don't use the words anyone or someone.

"People who sell skin care products will often say, 'I'm looking for anyone with skin.' They really do not want anyone who just has skin. A baby has skin. Do they want to do business with a baby? Of course they don't because a baby has no money; however, they requested this type of referral.

"Let's return to the example of a good referral for us. We would like to have fleet accounts. Just saying fleet accounts is too general. The more specific we are, the better our results will be.

"When we know the industry, then we say it. When we can narrow it down to a company, then we say it. If we can narrow it down to a position in the company, even better. If we can narrow it down to the person who occupies that position, then that is the best. I'll give you examples of what we're discussing. Ask for as specific a referral as you know. Each of the following examples gets more specific.

Example One:
"A great referral for us today is a company in the medical transport business.

Example Two:
"A great referral for us today is a company in the medical transport business by the name of Med South.

Example Three:
"A great referral for us today is the President of the medical transport company Med South.

Example Four:
"A great referral for us today is the President of the medical transport company Med South. His name is Brad Fulton."

Clark nodded his head in understanding.

"For a solid month, a member of a networking group asked for what she considered to be a specific referral. During the referral portion of her infomercial, she said, 'In the way of referrals, I'm looking for introductions to dentists.' Without fail, she asked for this same referral for one month. During this month, she received zero referrals.

"The next month, she narrowed down her referral request to a specific person. She said, 'In the way of referrals, I would like an introduction to the Dentist, Dr. Nurani, who has an office at 1030 Duluth Highway in Lawrenceville, Georgia. That day after the meeting, she received three referrals. Some of her fellow members said, 'I don't know Dr. Nurani, but I'll introduce you to my Dentist.' Although she had asked for introductions to Dentists for one solid month, she had received zero referrals.

"When she narrowed down her referral to a specific person that she wanted an introduction to, it helped her fellow networkers to focus on a specific person. For this purpose, we don't say we would like a referral to anyone who has a car. Most people of age and means will own at least one car. When we say the word anyone, our fellow members think of no one.

"Of the five components required for a breathtaking infomercial, this one is often overlooked. People would rather say their name and company name twice or ramble on about what they do than ask for a specific referral. The networking group will act as your sales team, but you have to train them on what kind of business you need. If you skip this portion because you don't practice or you ramble, you leave out a critical part of your infomercial. Do you have any questions about this part?"

"Do you mind if I practice this with you right now?" asked Clark.

"Not at all," answered Art. "That's why we are here."

"In the way of referrals, I'd like an introduction to Jim Johnson; who owns Johnson's Management Team, a property management company."

"Clark, it doesn't get any more specific than that. You seem to be a quick study."

"I'm trying," replied Clark. "I appreciate you breaking down the infomercial into segments and allowing me to get your input."

"Clark, how old are you?"

"As of two weeks ago I'm 50," answered Clark.

"Happy belated birthday!"

"Thank you."

"The reason I asked your age is because I want to ask you something. Do you remember who had the commercial that asked, 'Where's the beef?'"

"Yes. That would be Wendy's."

"That commercial has not aired for over 25 years, but people still remember the commercial. Why do you suppose that is?" asked Art.

"I don't know. Maybe it was the way those elderly ladies acted, and one of them asked, 'Where's the beef?'" replied Clark.

"That has a little bit to do with it, but the main reason for the success of that commercial and the reason it lingers in our minds is they had a great tag line or memory hook. A memory hook creates a picture in our mind associated with the individual who has the memory hook. An infomercial should have a memory hook/tag line that ties to the business or the person representing the business. Often when a person cannot remember a company name or the name of the company representative, they will remember the tag line. Since the name of our business is Nobody's, our tag line is: Like James Bond says, 'Nobody's does it better.' Clark, do you understand this part of the infomercial?"

"I think so, but I can't think of a tag line for our business. Do you suppose you could help me with that?" asked Clark.

"We can try. Once you have attended the networking meetings for a while, you may not need to use a tag line because the members will know you. You can use the few seconds that were previously used on the tag line on the supporting story for your LCD. When attending a meeting for the first few times, the tag line helps with your branding.

"We discussed business, but I never asked the name of your company."

"The name is A+ Pest Control."

"I like that name. The first tag line that comes to mind is, 'When it comes to termite and pest control, we make the best grade.' Another possible tag line is, 'A+ Pest Control delivers A+ service every time.' Find something that works and use it."

"I like those, Art."

"We've talked about the different parts of an infomercial. The amount of time that you are allowed determines which parts of the infomercial that you use. If you have 60 seconds, you can use all five parts."

Art took a sip of water then continued.

"Let's review the five components of an infomercial for thought process number 1:

1. Your name
2. Your company name
3. Your LCD and supporting facts or a story
4. A specific referral
5. Wrap up with your name and company name. If you have 60 seconds, add your tag line here

After seeing Clark nod his head, Art asked, "Do you have any questions?"

"Yes," answered Clark. "Will you give me your infomercial?"

"How much time do I have?"

"Will you give one that's approximately 60 seconds?"

"My name is Art Kleve, owner and operator of Nobody's. Nobody's is your one-stop, honest auto repair shop. Everybody is somebody at Nobody's. Our competition loves us, and you will, too. Midas will tell you that nobody beats Midas. Ford will tell you that nobody knows your Ford better. GM will tell you that nobody beats Mr. Goodwrench for service. Our customers will tell you that Nobody's beats everybody for quality, service and price. Our special this week is a free oil change with any additional paid service because a vehicle will last longer if the oil is changed on a regular basis. A great referral for us today is an introduction to Brad Fulton, the

President of the medical transport company Med South. We would love to service their fleet of vehicles. Be somebody, bring your vehicle to Nobody's, and like James Bond, you'll say, 'Nobody's does it better!'"

"Wow, Art! I knew that you were good with infomercials or Tim would have never connected me with you, but man, oh man, this is more than I expected. I am new to this, but will you allow me to practice an infomercial on you?"

"Yes, that is a good idea."

"It won't be polished like yours. My name is Clark with A+ Pest Control. We are in the termite and pest control industry. Termites cause millions of dollars of damage each year. Since it is termite swarm season, a great referral for me is your neighbor, Sally Jones, who called you in a panic and said, 'I have all of these flying bugs in my house, and they look like flying ants.' That is a great referral for us. When it comes to termite and pest control, we always make the best grade."

"Clark, that's excellent! Remember to practice, practice and practice some more."

Thought Process #2

"When using Thought Process 2, follow these steps: open, create pain, hook with a question and establish your company's product or services as providing the beneficial solution."

"After hitting someone with a sledge hammer and causing pain, I could ask, 'How bad does it hurt?' Is that what you want me to do?" laughed Clark.

"No. Let me explain."

After drinking another sip of water, Art continued.

"Let's analyze the four parts of this process.

1. Open – Talk about yourself and your company. I am Art Kleve, and we own Nobody's which is an automobile repair shop.
2. Create Pain – This is not physical pain but a painful situation. We work with people who have been told by other repair shops that their automobile needs costly repairs.
3. Hook – Have you or a loved one ever experienced a visit to an auto repair shop and the manager told you expensive repairs were needed for your automobile?
4. Solution – We do a diagnostic inspection on automobiles and then give the owner a report of our findings. We also let them know what repairs are needed now and which repairs can wait.

"What we have just discussed are two different ways of presenting infomercials when you attend a networking meeting, and you have at least 30 seconds. Some stupendous networkers prefer the first process, while others prefer the second. Pick one way and perfect it. You may want to use the second way at a meeting where you have not built the relationships yet and the first process for meetings after you have established some good relationships.

"Do you have any questions about this second thought process?"

"I don't think so."

"If you get together with someone at a meeting which has not started, or the meeting is a mixer where participants walk around introducing themselves to each other, tell someone you meet a benefit your company offers, instead of giving them your entire infomercial. Since this part of the meeting, or this type of meeting, is not geared toward infomercials, simply proclaim a benefit that your company provides.

"Mentioning a benefit your company provides has different names like unique selling point, value statement or benefit statement. For the sake of discussion, we will call it a benefit statement. Regardless of what one chooses to call it, the statement allows you to declare a benefit that hopefully interests the person with whom you are conversing. Instead of trying to explain your business, simply give a benefit of your business. If your benefit statement arouses their curiosity, they will ask you to tell them more about what you do.

"You are in the pest control industry, so if someone asks what you do, you could say, 'We provide homeowners peace of mind by protecting one of their most valuable assets.' A business coach may say, 'We help business owners achieve a higher level of success.'

"Clark, do you understand this?"

"I think so."

"It looks like Tim has arrived, and I have choir practice at 4:00 p.m. Clark, I have enjoyed our time together, and I wish you much success. Here is my card which has my cell number on it. Call me any time you feel like you need assistance with your infomercial."

"Art, I have also enjoyed our time together. Thanks for sharing your knowledge about infomercials."

"You are welcome."

On the drive back to Curt's, Tim asked, "How did your visit with Art go?"

"Sensational! That man seems to really understand infomercials. He said to practice so that I can take advantage of every opportunity to give an infomercial. I plan to practice this afternoon so that my infomercial has no kinks in it."

"That will help you perfect your networking skills," remarked Tim.

"He also taught me how to give a brief introduction with a benefit statement."

"Infomercials are just one part of networking. We'll learn more tomorrow. Let's meet at 8:00 a.m. at Curt's for breakfast. Afterwards, we'll drive to meet David Alexander.

"David is a well-known speaker and has co-authored several books. His latest best-selling book, co-authored with Dr. Ivan Misner and Brian Hillard entitled *Networking Like a Pro,* has aided many business professionals in the improvement of their networking skills. He involves himself in a total of 18 different businesses, some of which are: High Achievers Network, a training company for business professionals, the BNI franchises for approximately half of North Carolina and the BNI franchises for most of Georgia."

"I know that we have completed only two days of the week-long program, but already my cup overflows. I can tell that this program will be for my betterment. Words can't describe my appreciation for how you are guiding me through all of this. Thank you."

"It's my privilege. I will see you in the morning."

CHAPTER 4

Presentations

On Monday at 8:00 a.m., Clark and Tim met at Curt's and ate breakfast which consisted of two eggs over medium, ham and toast.

"As soon as we finish, we'll drive down the road to meet David," explained Tim. "We are scheduled to meet him at 10:30 a.m."

"Tim, if you don't mind, I'd like for you to listen to my two different infomercials and also my benefit statement."

"Alright."

During the drive, Clark and Tim talked about various topics, and Tim listened intently while Clark verbalized his infomercials.

"My name is Clark with A+ Pest Control. We service both residential and commercial properties for termite and pest control in the 14-county metro area. This time of year, many people battle Argentine ants which can have multiple queens producing thousands of ants per day. Entomologists tell us that a person will only see 1-3 percent of an ant colony. We recently treated the home of a man who had tried to treat the ant problem himself for six years. He had millions of ants. In two treatments, we took care of his ant problem. Today, a great referral for us is your neighbor, Sally Jones, who has complained about having a constant ant problem. When it comes to pest control, we always make the best grade."

"Tim, that's the first one, now for the second."

"Clark, hold on just a second. Do you want me to comment on them after you finish each one or wait until you complete all of them?"

"It doesn't matter to me, whichever way works best for you."

"I will hold my comments until the end. If you feel like you need to discuss any element, just stop. Continue with your second infomercial."

"I'm Clark with A+ Pest Control. Our company controls the pest population for homes and commercial structures. We generally work with homeowners and business owners who are overrun with small ants. Have you or someone close to you ever felt like the star in the movie *Invasion of the Ants?* We can come to your home or business and rid your place of those unwanted guests.

"Ok, Tim. That's number two.

"Now, here's my benefit statement:

"We provide homeowners peace of mind by protecting one of their most valuable assets."

"Clark, it sounds to me like you spent a few hours practicing. Keep that up, and in no time at all you'll be a champion networker."

In what seemed like a few minutes, they arrived at David's office.

"David, how good to see you again," declared Tim as he put out his hand to greet David. "This is Clark. He's the young man that I told you about last week."

David shook Clark's hand and said, "Clark, how are you?"

"I'm fine, and how are you," asked Clark.

"Superb," answered David.

"Clark, I need to run a few errands. I'll return in a couple of hours, and we'll head back towards the house."

David and Clark walked into a nice conference room and had a seat in the comfortable rolling chairs.

"Tim told me that you have a pest control business."

"That's correct."

"Even though my wife and I need a quality company to provide termite protection for our home, we will not do business with someone unless we have known him or her for a long time or we have a recommendation from someone in our network. I personally know several people who are like me. They will not do business with someone they do not know, unless they are endorsed by someone that they know and in whom they have confidence. Based upon the strong recommendation of Tim, we'd like to talk to you about your services.

"As a matter of fact, I have so much confidence in Tim, that if he told me to jump off a cliff and he would catch me, I would do it. He has been there for me on many occasions. This shows the power of relationships built on trust. Many such relationships begin through the vehicle called networking."

"We work in the area, and we'd love the opportunity to earn your business."

"Give me a call next week, and we'll schedule an appointment for an estimate."

"We'll do it," replied Clark.

"Let's discuss the next topic that will support you in becoming a networking guru. I believe Art Kleve taught you about infomercials. Out of all the people that I've ever heard, he has one of the best infomercials. How did that go?"

"Incredible! Art gave me excellent information on how to give an effective infomercial."

"Do you feel like you have a handle on that aspect?"

"I practiced on Art and later on Tim. They both seemed to think I understand."

"Well, if Tim thinks it is good, then that means you have it down. Tim is not called the networking guru for nothing. If a networker will use the system, the benefits are astronomical.

"Clark, normally once a person has been in a networking group for 2-6 months, they will have the opportunity to give a 7-10 minute presentation.

"All presentations of any type should follow a formula that I learned from my good friend, Doug Grady, who is the President of High Achievers. The formula called A.W.P.C. can be adapted for a presentation of any length.

"*A* stands for approach. As you approach any presentation, have you evaluated your subject matter thoroughly and are you prepared to use the appropriate vernacular for your audience. In other words, have you done your homework?

"*W* stands for warmup. This is your presentation's opening and sets the stage for your success. Have a strong opening like a personal, compelling and emotional story. Even a comical story related to your presentation works.

"*P* stands for presentation which is the main portion of your presentation. I will speak more on this a little later. One quick note here; only use two or three points. Keep it simple.

"*C* stands for close. This is your call to action. I personally don't like to think about this as a close. To me close ends a relationship, kind of like closing a door. So I'm going to use the letter *N* for next step. Always give your audience a next step which is a way to begin a relationship with you.

"Speaking of next step, let's discuss a few tips to get you started.

"Have energy when you present. Don't act like you need to drink Red Bull or Five Hour Energy.

"Dress for the occasion. You are a business professional, so dress like one. You really don't want to show up at the meeting looking like you just woke up, or you just slopped hogs.

"Don't use professional jargon. If you present to a group of industry professionals, then it's appropriate to use professional jargon, but not when speaking to a mixed audience.

"If you plan to use a technology device, such as a computer or a projector, arrive early for the meeting to make sure it works correctly. Know your presentation well enough that if the computer or projector quits working, you can continue with your presentation. I've seen people give a presentation and in the middle of it the computer quits working, and they are lost. They would spend 3-4 minutes of their allotted time trying to reboot the computer and program. It becomes a big debacle when that happens.

"If you plan to pass out materials, give them out at the end of your presentation. When you put out brochures or reading material in advance, people will read your material instead of listening to what you have to say. The exception to this would be if your presentation includes a worksheet where the attendees fill in the blanks.

"Many times people do not understand the purpose of a presentation at a networking meeting. I have listened to more than a few people tell the audience how they do their job.

"An example of this related to your business would be if you told us, 'We use a sprayer that has 25 psi which allows our product to penetrate cracks. Without this kind of pressure, the pesticide does not make it to the proper destination.' In my research of pesticides, I also discovered that there are different mixtures. You could also talk about a suspended concentrate versus baits or the potency of one product over another. This educates your audience, but the purpose of your presentation in a networking environment is to generate more referrals. Don't tell us how you do your job. We don't need a five-minute education on how to kill roaches grave-yard dead. You want to tell us how we can refer potential customers to you.

"Clark, do you have any questions thus far?"

"I don't have any questions related to what you have explained, but may I ask a question pertaining to another topic?"

"Certainly."

"May I use your restroom?"

"Yes. When you walk toward the entrance of the suite, it's the second door on the left."

"Thanks. I will return in a couple of minutes."

After Clark returned, David asked if he would like something to drink.

"Yes. What do you have?"

"Since I compete in triathlons and am very health conscious, we usually have bottled water or fruit juice. Let's look in the refrigerator. Occasionally, our office manager, Cindy, will stock some type of soda. She's running errands right now, but if we don't have what you want, she will be happy to pick up your favorite drink."

When David opened the refrigerator, he saw several bottles of water, two cartons of kiwi juice, two cans of Pepsi, four cans of Diet Coke and three cans of Mountain Dew. He told Clark the choices, and he decided on a Mountain Dew.

"Thanks for the drink."

"You are welcome. Let's continue."

"Clark, how would you like to gain an extra 3-5 minutes on a presentation?"

"David, I'll be honest with you, I probably could not give a two-minute presentation at this time. I don't see how an extra few minutes could help me."

"Clark, I understand how you feel; however, when we finish today, I believe you will be more confident and have a structure for your time. Then you could give an hour-long presentation."

"David, I don't think you would lie to me, so I'll just have to rely on you. When I become proficient at giving my presentation, it will be wonderful to have the extra time."

"You want to take advantage of every minute. A speaker should have a typed bio. Do this in advance. When a person does not have a well-prepared bio, the group does not know much about the speaker unless the speaker spends some of his or her time giving the bio. Your bio should be 1-2 minutes in length.

"If the person who would normally introduce the speaker is not well-spoken, ask if someone else can introduce you. With a well-written bio, you can spend that time when you would talk about yourself better preparing your sales team to find you referrals. This is where you gain one or two minutes on your presentation because you don't take away from your presentation talking about yourself.

"Once the presentation has been organized and practiced, you may save enough time to spend a minute on a quick synopsis of what makes you different from your competition.

"Clark, have you ever heard the saying, 'Facts tell, but stories sell?'"

"No," answered Clark. "Will you explain what that means?"

"Sure," answered David. "Facts are facts. They can impart information about goods or services, but the facts don't really sell. They simply give details about the products or services; however, stories about those goods or services engage people's emotions. When people become emotionally involved in the story and can personally relate or know someone who can relate to the problem that you solved, it contributes to the selling of your product or service.

"When you spent time with Art, did he talk to you about LCD's?"

"Yes. He said when giving an infomercial to focus on one LCD and tell a story about it."

"Well, think of this in the same vein, but instead of using one LCD, you will use two or three. Whether you use two or three LCD's depends on the amount of time you have. If you are giving a 7-minute presentation, you may want to use two, but if you are giving a 10-minute presentation, then use three.

"Spend 1-2 minutes on an LCD and telling a story about how you helped someone with a particular problem or need.

"Next, tell your sales team that when one of their friends, co-workers or family members mention they are having a similar need to bring you up in the conversation.

"Always remember that your audience at a networking group is your sales team. Educate them on how they can help you. Don't try to sell to them, but sell through them.

"Let me give you an example in my business. Besides speaking across the Country at various events and owning BNI franchises in Georgia and North Carolina, we own a training company. If I'm giving a 10-minute presentation at a closed networking I want to tell people what kind of referrals we need and how to open the door for specific referrals, not how we train."

Clark nodded his head as the picture became clearer.

"'In our training company, we teach our customers how to have phenomenal growth. We are not just interested in earning a paycheck. We want them to apply what we impart so their business can grow. We follow up in one week, two weeks, one month, two months, six months and one year to make sure the concepts that we teach are being followed.

"'We recently worked with a client who previously had not reached any of his goals. After just four months of working with us, he surpassed his goals for the entire year. One referral that we would like to have is an introduction to your CPA. CPA's have clients who are business owners at various stages.

"'We'll pretend the name of the CPA is Kevin. The way you can introduce us is by saying, 'Kevin, do you have any business clients that may be stuck in a rut but would like to grow well beyond where they are?' When he says 'yes,' tell him, 'I know a man that has a magnificent training company that works with business owners to obtain the results that they desire. Business owners and employees who follow the concepts taught by his company average 30 percent growth. His company even has a money-back guarantee. Kevin, I know you want to see that your business clients are highly successful. Will it be ok if I have David give you a call?'

"'Other businesses that we would like the opportunity to serve are financial firms like Mitchell Investment Group. If you know Mark Mitchell, the President, or the President of another investment firm, we'd like an introduction. The way for you to introduce us to one of these individuals is to say: 'How would you like to increase the sales of your firm? I know you probably have some kind of sales training, but I know a man with a marvelous training company that has worked with many companies in the metro area to increase sales by an average of 30 percent. Wouldn't that be great? I'll have David give you a call if that's ok. What would work best, today at 4:00 p.m. or tomorrow at 9:00 a.m.?'"

"Wow, David! That was amazing!"

"Thanks. It has been practiced hundreds of times."

David continued, "At most networking meetings that I have attended when the speaker finishes the presentation the person in charge of the meeting will say, 'Does anyone have questions?' Sometimes, admirable questions will be asked, and at other times, members will ask misaligned questions. To avoid less-than-ideal questions, plant your questions."

"David, what do you mean when you say to plant questions?"

"In advance of your meeting, type out three questions and give them to three different members. Ask each member to raise his or her hand at question time and ask the specific question on their sheet. These questions allow you the opportunity to educate your sales team concerning one-three more of your best targeted referrals. When people raise their hands to ask questions, only call on the three members to whom you gave a question.

"You may have several who raise their hands to ask a question, but only call on those with whom you planted a question. This is where you add an additional two or three minutes to your presentation."

Clark responded with an enthusiastic, "I understand! I understand!"

"Some examples of questions and answers that I plant are:

Planted Question One:

"Since many times a brand new company has little capital, do you have an affordable plan to help the new business owner?"

Answer One:

"What a splendid question. When we began the training company, we decided we would have a plan for new business owners whereby they could pay as they go. Our guarantee says they do not pay at all if within six months of beginning our training program if they have followed our system and they have not benefited from our training to the point that they have tripled their investment. We are that confident in the training that we have developed. New companies less than one year old are excellent referrals for us."

Planted Question Two:

"David, a friend of mine is considering opening a business. When is the best time to put him in contact with you?"

Answer Two:

"Friday at 2:00 p.m. would be a good time for their free consultation. If they are in the consideration phase of starting a new business, then we want to make sure they begin correctly. Most businesses fail within five years. We'd like to help them understand all aspects of the business and connect them to people who can ensure things are set up correctly. Thanks for that wonderful question."

Planted Question Three:

"David, do you only work in the metro area because I have a cousin that owns a business in the northeast corner of the State?"

Answer Three:

"Chad, that's a fantastic question. We train in person, via webinars and via our secure proprietary members' only website. For the face-to-face portion of our training, I will go to their location, or they can come to the office. The rest happens via the internet. We can train anywhere in the World.

"When it's question time, I may only have enough time for one. That one question still creates one more referral opportunity for my sales team to look for on my behalf. Does that make sense to you, Clark?"

"I think so. Do you think we have time for me to work on my presentation?"

"We do; however, before we work on it, there's one more thing to cover," David said. "Some networking groups require that when you are the presenter you bring a door prize, but with other groups, it is optional. I recommend that any time you give a presentation, you bring a door prize. A door prize should cost approximately $25.

"Don't give someone a discount off your service or offer them some evaluation process that you normally give away as a door prize. Even though members know at least one month in advance that they are scheduled to give their presentation, the typical door prize consists of stopping by a convenience store on the way to the meeting and purchasing a $25 gas card. That takes quite a bit of thought. I'm kidding.

"Clark, put more thought into your door prize than buying one at the last minute. When people say that Thanksgiving snuck up on me, I just want to say, 'You're kidding. Did they change the day this year and forget to tell you?' Don't be like that. Be prepared.

"When a new member presents to his or her networking group, a phenomenal way to quickly establish good will is to buy a product or service from another member of the group for approximately $25 and give it away as a door prize.

"I learned this principle from Tim. When he speaks at the Chamber of Commerce, he wants everyone to have a door prize so he orders almond crème cheese cupcakes from a fellow member. Cakes made by Cakes with a Plan are off- the-charts delicious, and she makes him enough cupcakes for the members who attend and some extra for the staff members. He spends approximately $100 every time he speaks at the Chamber."

"That's a great idea," remarked Clark.

"It sure is. He does not announce this, but I know for a fact that he does it. When he speaks at a closed networking meeting, he usually buys a certificate from the auto mechanic for an oil change, a head shot from the photographer, a massage from the massage therapist or something similar to give away as the door prize.

"One time he had a life coach in his networking group, and he asked her if she had some product or service she would sell him to give away as a door prize. She told him she had a baseline evaluation service that sells for $100, but she would sell it to him for $22. She made him a certificate, and he gave that away for his door prize. The recipient of the door prize used it for a family member, and the quality of life for the individual improved drastically as a result of counseling sessions that began with the door prize. Clark, does this make sense?"

"Yes. When you're the presenter at a meeting, always have a door prize, and if possible, use a product or service from a fellow member."

"Sounds like you have it. We have a few more minutes, so we can spend the time that we have left on your presentation. What's the first thing you should do, Clark?"

"Type a bio."

"Correct. Once you have your presentation ready, practice, practice and practice some more. Try to have a fellow member listen to your presentation in advance and give you tips. Tell the member to be honest with you because you want to give a stunning presentation. Don't ever deliver a presentation and stumble over your words.

"One day you may hear a presentation, and the first words they'll say are, 'I didn't have much time to prepare. I was asked to do this at the last minute.'

"Don't ever fall into that trap. It would be best to have three or four presentations ready at all times that you have practiced. If you are asked to speak about your business, you can give your speech at a moment's notice. Now give me some ideas about how you would start your presentation," finished David.

Clark began, "At A+ Pest Control we are more interested in the welfare of our customers and potential customers than we are their pocketbooks. We always strive to do what is best for each person. Sometimes people would like to switch to our company, but if it would be best for them to stay with their current company, that is what we advise them to do."

David stated "Your opening is good. You're telling your sales team how you are different from other companies. Continue with the next part."

Clark continued, "I'd like to spend a few minutes on what would be good referrals for our company. Approximately six months ago, we were introduced to Karen from KPP Properties. Insects and spiders invaded several of their commercial buildings, and the company that they had used for several years couldn't control the problem. We evaluated some of their buildings, wrote out a treatment plan and began treatment. Karen has been overjoyed. Approximately one month ago, they turned over several other properties to our company. Since we are trying to grow our commercial business, we would like an introduction to the CEO of NCR, Ronnie Jones. We would love the opportunity to serve them for their pest control and termite control needs.

"Another company that has a facility close to NCR's location is McKesson. We would like an introduction to their CEO, Nathan Smith, as well. The best way to introduce us is to ask him if they have a current pest control company and if he is happy with them. If he says, 'Yes!' then ask him if he ever noticed spider webs around the front entry. When he says, 'Yes!' then tell him you know of a company that will keep those spider webs wiped down which will give their building a better appearance. If he says, 'No!' ask if they ever experience any kind of pest problems. Tell him you know the owner of a company that is fantastic at controlling the pest population of commercial buildings," finished Clark.

"Clark, you seem to have the gist of the information you need to give during a 7-10 minute presentation. Do you have any questions?"

"David, would I stop at two specific names of people associated with commercial properties, or do I ask for others? The reason that I ask is I have heard of an up and coming concrete and paving company, and I would like to meet the owner.

"I've heard that their quality of work speaks for itself, and in the next few years, they will be a major player in the concrete and paving industry. I'd like to make the connection while they are a smaller company. Since he will probably be paving the parking lots or pouring concrete for some large commercial facilities, I'd like to connect with him. He may be able to get us in the door for pest control at the same commercial buildings."

"Clark, you can mention two-three specific contacts who you would like an introduction to. I would not reference more because it becomes too difficult to keep up with more than three. Since I have a large network, by chance, I might know the owner and would be happy to make the introduction for you. What is the owner's name, and what is the name of his company?"

"His name is William Voan, and his company's name is Ascon Paving. Although they are a local company, I've heard they have worked as far away as California."

"I don't know him personally, but I have heard of him. I will find out if any of my contacts know him personally and would be willing to make that introduction. Let's continue. "If you are giving a presentation about your business to a networking group of which you are not a member, you may adjust things somewhat. Tell the audience more about your company and share stories about how you have worked with others who have experienced the same problems that they encounter.

"Our time has quickly come and gone. Before Tim whisks you away, I'd like to recap what we have discussed:

1. Have energy.
2. Dress for the occasion.
3. Don't use professional jargon.
4. Before the meeting begins, if you plan to use technology devices such as a laptop or overhead projector, make sure they are functioning properly. If

they quit working for any reason, continue without them.

5. If using printed materials, pass them out after the presentation.
6. In advance, give the person who will introduce you a well-written bio of 1-2 minutes in length.
7. Briefly tell what separates you from your competition or a mission statement.
8. Use two-three LCD's, telling stories about each.
9. Ask for referrals related to the LCD's that you use.
10. For question and answer time, plant your questions.
11. Bring a door prize.

"That about wraps it up," David announced. "Good luck to you!"

"David, I sure do appreciate your time. I will do my best to make you proud of me. Maybe one day when it's my time to give a presentation, you'll be there to hear me and see if I have it down like you do. I can hardly wait," finished Clark.

"Clark, I think in no time at all, you'll have these presentation skills down to a science."

He stood up as Tim entered the conference room.

"Hello, Tim, did you finish all of your errands?"

"I sure did. While out and about, I ran into Joe Lynch, President of Onyx Stone, a financial advisement group. After we talked for a few minutes, he told me that he wants you to call him for some training. His name and number are on his card." Tim handed David a business card.

In expressing his gratitude, David responded with, "Thanks, Tim! You are truly the networking guru."

"How did the session go with Clark?" asked Tim.

"I think it went well. What do you think, Clark?"

"Definitely," voiced Clark. "David enlightened me on the purpose of a 7-10 minute presentation in a networking group. I'll work on this because like Tim said, 'I need to perfect my networking craft and each portion of it.'"

"Thanks, David, for educating Clark and for your continued friendship."

On the return trip, Tim and Clark discussed what David had taught him. In what seemed like a few minutes, they had returned to Curt's.

"Let's meet again tomorrow morning at 8:00 a.m. for breakfast, and then we'll go to the law office of David Lawler," Tim said. "He began his business as a real estate closing attorney. When that market slowed down, he expanded his firm to general practice, where he handles everything from adoptions to wills; however, he does not handle bankruptcy cases. Besides being a skillful attorney, he is one of the wittiest people you'll ever meet and has a heart of gold. I'll see you in the morning."

CHAPTER 5

Referrals

On Tuesday morning Tim and Clark met for breakfast as planned. After eating a breakfast consisting of country ham, eggs, biscuits and coffee, they made the 30-minute trip to the law office of David Lawler.

"Hello, David, how are you today?" asked Tim.

"Well, I am blessed and highly favored."

"David, this is my friend, Clark. Do you still have all of the Star Wars memorabilia?"

"Yes. As a matter of fact, come back to my office, and I'll show you some of it. I have a surprise for you, as well. Do you remember that I wanted to buy a vintage Peavey bass guitar?"

"Yes, I remember that," replied Tim.

"Well, I was finally able to purchase the one that I have wanted for years," declared David.

"If you have it here, I'd love to see it."

David took it out of the case and handed it to Tim.

"David, I like it. I like it. How does it sound?"

"Hold on a minute. I'll plug it up and play a song for you," answered David.

"David, I am happy for you. That is one nice bass guitar, and it has a great jazzy sound."

"I agree. The pickups on this bass are of the highest quality."

"Ok, guys," announced Tim. "I'm going to meet Art at his shop, and I'll be back in a couple of hours."

"Clark, tell me what you have learned so far about networking."

"Tim taught me about the system; and Art Kleve taught me how to give an outstanding infomercial. He said to make sure to include the key components every time. He has a fabulous infomercial."

"How well I know! Art and I have been friends for many years."

"David Alexander taught me about giving an excellent 7-10 minute presentation," responded Clark.

"I don't know whether you realize this or not, but those men are some of the most astute business men and best networkers in the Country, not just in the metro area.

"Clark, why do you suppose anyone would join a networking organization?" asked David.

"I think the main reason would be to grow their business," answered Clark.

"That answer would be correct. Many times people will come to a networking meeting with wrong ideas, misconceptions or bad networking habits learned from people who never understood the purpose of networking. Some of the misconceptions are: people think it is a buyer's club, a dog and pony show, a moneymaking scheme for the organization or they approach networking with a me-first attitude. People will walk into a group and expect to receive business right away.

"They approach networking just like a hunter does. A hunter goes to the field, shoots his prey, and then has meat for a little while. People go to a networking meeting with the same psyche; they want to go to the meeting, make a sale and then go celebrate for a while.

"Networking should be approached with the mentality of a farmer who realizes that it will take some time, but he will be able to feed his family for a much longer period. Clark, I remember when I was a child that we had a garden. The first thing we did was plow the area where we planted our crop. Then we planted the seeds or seedlings. After a few weeks, my Mama would tell me and my siblings to go pull the weeds out of the garden. The next day it seemed like the same weeds that we had pulled the previous day miraculously showed up again. As a child, I learned to hate pulling those weeds because I didn't particularly like many of the things that grew in the garden. I enjoyed potatoes and a few beans, like butter beans, but I didn't like green beans because they are really just a hull. The life lessons learned from farming have stuck with me all these years."

"Tim basically said the same thing when he talked about the system," replied Clark. "Did you all take a Networking 101 class, and that's what they taught?"

"No, but when you're explaining the concepts of networking, the differences between farming and hunting are a good way to illustrate the point.

"According to Webster's, the definition for referral is the act of sending someone to another person or place for treatment, help, or advice.

"Some organizations say that they pass referrals when what they really pass are leads. I'll give you an example of a lead versus a referral. I drive into a neighborhood and see that a house needs to be painted, but I don't know the owner of the house. If I tell my painter friend about the house, then I have passed a lead.

"Now, imagine I am at someone's home and see that it needs to be painted. I ask if they plan to have their house painted in the near future, and they say, 'Yes.' Next, I ask if they have a painter. If they don't, I'll ask if it's ok to have the best painter in the area give them a call. If they say, 'Yes,' I have passed a referral when I give their contact information to the painter. You don't want leads, and you don't want to pass leads. Referrals are so much better.

"You met David Alexander yesterday; he co-wrote a fantastic book called *Networking Like a Pro.* In that book, he talks about 10 different levels of referrals. The higher the level of referral, the higher the closing percentage is. For me, the best way to describe levels of referrals is like this.

"Bronze level: A couple wants to have their house painted, and you give them the painter's business card.

"Silver level: A couple wants to have their house painted, and you ask if it is ok to have the painter call them.

"Gold level: A couple wants to have their house painted, and you call the painter and have him talk to them while you are with them.

"Platinum level: A couple wants to have their house painted, and you give the painter a face-to-face introduction.

"I should have asked earlier, but do you want something to drink?"

"What do you have?"

"We have bottled water, Coke, Pepsi, Mountain Dew, Dr. Pepper, Diet Pepsi and Sprite."

"I'd like to have a Pepsi."

David walked out of his office and into his kitchen, opened the refrigerator and picked up a Pepsi for Clark and a bottle of water for himself. After returning to his office, he gave Clark his drink and sat down at his desk.

"Thanks, David."

"You're welcome. Let's continue.

"People have needs, and many times they do not know who to call. They may look on the internet, at a magazine and possibly in a phone book. In case you have not figured it out, not everyone who advertises has the potential client's best interest at heart. Many business owners or professionals are concerned about making a sale, and if there is a possibility of selling multiple services or upselling services even if they are not needed, then that is what they will do. When dealing with people, try to do what is best for the person and not what is best for you or your company. Let me give you some examples."

Example 1

"When people want to open a business, the type of entity that makes me the most money would be a Subchapter C Corporation. They may only need to operate as a Limited Liability Corporation, which commonly goes by the initials LLC which makes me the least amount of money. I will give them all of the available options in which they can set up their business, and based upon how they answer certain questions, I will give them a recommendation as to what would be best for them."

Example 2

"When someone comes to me asking for help with a divorce, the best thing for me financially is a heated and much disputed divorce case; however, I will only take a divorce case if there has been abuse, neglect or unfaithfulness. Divorce hurts everyone, especially the children. The life expectancy of a divorcee drops by approximately seven years. If someone comes to me and says I don't love him or her anymore or we just can't get along, I advise them to seek marriage counseling.

"When one spouse has been unfaithful, and the other spouse desires to proceed with a divorce, then we do our best to resolve it quickly. The couple may have $100,000 in assets. If we can resolve it quickly and meet somewhere in the middle, they may end up with $92,000 worth of assets to divide; however, if it drags out for a few weeks then they may only have $60,000 worth of assets remaining. Attorneys are paid for their time, so the longer that a divorce case lasts, the more I get paid. A long divorce case usually doesn't bode well for my client."

"David, if I understand you correctly, you don't try to milk your clients for every dime," interjected Clark.

"Clark, you would be 100 percent correct in that analysis. I would rather a divorce client spend $4,000, have quick resolution and give my card out to 10 other people than he or she spend $20,000 with me and tell others that I took advantage of him or her.

"When looking to meet the needs of people, always listen. Most people were born with two ears and one mouth. That simple fact should tell people to listen twice as much as they talk. Listen for needs wherever you are.

"You could be in line at the grocery store, and the man in front of you mentions to the clerk that his back has been hurting for a week. Tell him that you know a chiropractor who has helped relieve the back pain of many people, and then give him the contact information such as the doctor's name, office number and address.

"You may be at your son's baseball game, and one of the other parents may tell you that they have weeds in the yard that won't die. Ask that parent if it would be ok to have your weed control person give them a call.

"An unwritten law exists about results in life. People who attend Church know it as 'You reap what you sow.' Another group of people may know it as 'what goes around, comes around' while others may know it as 'the law of reciprocity.' Basically what this law says is if you give, you will receive. If you are kind, then you will receive kindness; if you deal with people deceitfully, then people will deal with you deceitfully. If you treat people right, then people will treat you right. Far too many people never learn this concept. Many people think only about themselves.

"Too many are takers and not givers, so they never learn that it is more blessed to give than to receive. I once heard a man say that if your hand is always closed because you're trying to hold onto what you have, then nothing else can be put into your hand. Clark, do you understand this very valuable concept?"

"I think so. Without saying it directly, you are saying I need to learn to give."

"Let me tell you something about Tim that he may never tell you. He and his wife give money to at least 15 charities every year. Additionally, they donate many hours of their time to charities."

"Wow! Tim is quite the man," proclaimed Clark.

"Yes, he is," acknowledged David. "All those who know him, love him and trust him immensely."

"In all of the different networking groups that I have attended, I found out that the average networker expects to receive a boat load of referrals, but they don't give that many themselves. The average networker passes 1-2 referrals per month; the good networker passes 4-5 per month; but the great networker will pass at least 10 per month.

"I have a friend, Jamie Harrelson, who lives in the Kernersville, North Carolina area. She works as a Realtor and averages giving out 25-35 referrals per month. This young lady happens to be a top producer for passing referrals in all of North Carolina and one of the top in the United States. In a few minutes, I will show you a system where you can average at least 10 referrals per month."

"David, that would be amazing," exclaimed Clark. "I understand this networking business might be new to me, but I think that would make me a powerful networker. Do you suppose we could talk Jamie into relocating to our area? According to what you said about a great networker passing on average 10 referrals per month, she has to be off the charts awesome if she passes 25-35. Is there another name for someone that good at passing referrals? She has to be the referral Wonder Woman!"

"If we could somehow talk Jamie into moving here, she would be an excellent referral partner for you. She would probably refer a minimum of $35,000 worth of business to you every year."

"Since she is your friend, please try to talk her into it," said Clark. "I have only made $5,000 in six months."

"Although it would be a privilege to have her in Georgia, once Tim finishes working with you and with what you are about to learn, you can be another Jamie in this area," announced David.

"Where I am right now, that's hard to believe, but I will trust you."

"I don't know about you, but approximately five times a week we receive phones calls where the caller desires a price for a service that we offer," proclaimed David. "At the end of the conversation, either the office manager or I will say if you ever need a service besides an attorney, let me know because I meet regularly with approximately 150 business owners who will offer you the same quality of service that we will.

"If the caller states a need then we tell him or her that we will have the particular business professional call. An example would be if the caller says I need someone to replace my water heater, then we say, 'I'll have Derrick with Royal Flush Plumbing give you a call. He is the best.' I really like his memory hook, too, 'A royal flush is better than a full house.' Usually everyone with whom you have a conversation will need another service besides the one that you offer.

"On one particular occasion, I was just about to leave the office to go to my weekly meeting, and I only had two referrals for the week. I talked with a potential customer on the phone, and when I finished with my speech, he said, 'I'm moving. Do you know a mover?' I replied, 'Yes. Is it ok for me to have him call you?' He responded with, 'Yes.' He also asked if I knew a painter and a landscaper to which I replied, 'Yes' and asked if it was ok to have both call and he said, 'Yes.' Instead of going to the meeting with two referrals, I went to the meeting with five.

"A system that we use around here is that anytime we meet with a customer or potential customer face to face, we use the same speech that we do when talking to someone on the phone at the end of the conversation: 'If you ever need anything besides an attorney, let me know because we meet regularly with approximately 150 business owners who will offer you the same quality of service that we will.' Then we take it a step beyond that by also adding: 'Let me show you a few of their business cards.'

"We then open our card caddy and begin to show the cards for the members of our network, and for each card we point to it and give the name of the person, the name of the company and a 30-second testimonial. This takes us a few minutes with each person, but we have had customers or potential customers need up to seven additional services. We have found that this approach aids the members of our network, but it benefits us more because we are assisting our clients in other areas of need, as well.

"Too many people in business care about the sale instead of the person. When we open up our card file of trusted business professionals to people who come to our office, they realize that we care more about them as a person than we do their pocketbook. If you win the person, you will win their pocketbook. If you are only concerned about their pocketbook, you may make the sale, but as soon as someone else comes along with a cheaper price, they will leave you. They will stay with you for a long time if you care about them more than their pocketbook.

"Years ago, I attended a seminar, and John Maxwell said, 'People don't care how much you know until they know how much you care.' One of the greatest lessons that I learned from my Mom that still impacts me today is that regardless of the product or service you sell, you are in the people business. Clark, if you will always do what is best for your customers, you will have a very successful business. Though we all live busy lives, we don't need to be so busy we can't take the time to lend a hand to others in need.

"Do you have any questions?"

"Not really. You have covered it well enough that it is resonating with me," responded Clark.

"Clark, I spoke to you about how to pass several referrals, but when it comes to receiving referrals, you would rather have a few good referral sources or partners than the referrals themselves. Let me give you an example. Since you are in pest control, a good referral partner for you would be a very productive Realtor because he or she could put you in contact with many people who need pest control and possibly termite control. Realtors show homes to new people in the area who do not have a relationship with a pest control company already. They could introduce your company as the company to call upon for pest control and termite control needs.

"Someone else that would be a good referral partner for you is a property management company. They will be able to put you in contact with many owners who can use your services. Clark, do you understand?"

"Yes. Let me ask you a question. Would a company that treats lawns for weeds be a good referral source for us?"

"They could be, but it would take more work than a Realtor or property manager," answered David. "Realtors and property managers see people face to face or talk to them on a regular basis. Weed control employees meet customers initially, but most of the time when they spray lawns, they leave without talking to the customer. Now, it would be helpful to you if they were willing to attach some of your information to the invoice they leave for the customer. Introducing you to their customers in their next mailing would be even more helpful. When they do their regular follow-up phone calls to their customers, you would receive an even higher level of referral if they gave you a testimonial at the end.

"Let me demonstrate how that phone call would sound: 'Mrs. Jones, this is Joe with Perfect Earth weed control. How are you? I just called to make sure that the weed control is going according to plan and that your lawn looks good. That's great. I also wanted to tell you that if you ever have an ant or termite problem, I know this phenomenal local pest control company that treats my home. They have knowledgeable and courteous technicians who care about their customers. I trust this company so much that they have a key to my home. When they call the night before to remind me they are coming, they treat my home and leave me the invoice on the kitchen table if I can't be there. In my opinion, they are the best in our area.'"

David sipped some water as he continued, "If a weed control company is willing to go the extra mile, then they could be a great referral source. Without it, they may pass the occasional referral but probably would not pass regular, useful referrals."

"Thanks, David, for the explanation. I understand what you mean."

Tim knocked on David's door, and Clark opened it.

Tim asked, "Are you guys finished?"

"Almost."

"I'll wait in the lobby until you have finished. I need to return some phone calls." Tim closed the door behind him.

"Clark, I can't stress enough that if you meet the needs of the people, they will remain loyal to you even when someone comes with a cheaper price. If you only concentrate on the sale and not on meeting your customers' needs, they'll drop you when they get a chance," finished David.

"David, I am surely indebted to you for all the knowledge and business insight you have shared with me."

"It has been my pleasure. Keep in touch."

"I will, and thanks again. I don't want Tim to wait any longer. He has been so kind to me."

"You are certainly blessed to have him take you under his wing and help you," stated David.

"I agree."

As they drove back to his car, Clark excitedly recapped what David Lawler had taught him about passing referrals.

"Tim, David said there was a Realtor from North Carolina who passes 25-35 referrals per month. I think he said her name was Jamie. Do you know her?"

"Yes. She happens to be one of the many friends that I have in my network."

"From David's description, in the networking world she is like a superstar. Would it be possible to meet her one day?"

"We don't have that in the agenda for this week, but stay true to what you learn this week. In a few months, I'll not only introduce you to her, but we'll have lunch with her. They have a barbeque place in Greensboro close to where Jamie lives that has some of the best barbeque that I have ever eaten. The owner of Boss Hog's Bar-B-Que happens to be the cousin of a good friend."

"Tim, I plan to stay true to what I learn because it will make me a better business owner. I now have another incentive, and that's to meet Jamie."

"Clark, when that day comes it will definitely be a pleasure for you. Although she passes a tremendous amount of referrals and is a networking superstar, she remains humble, and you will not encounter a nicer person in the World."

"We have returned to your car. Let's have breakfast in the morning at 7:00 a.m. We have a long drive, and we will meet your next teacher for lunch."

"That sounds good to me, Tim. I will see you then."

CHAPTER 6

Sharing Knowledge

On Wednesday morning after enjoying a breakfast of pancakes, bacon and milk, Tim and Clark drove to Charlotte, N.C. to meet with Gina Herald. During the drive to Charlotte, Tim asked Clark to recap what he had been taught so far.

"It's a good thing that we have a few miles to travel because it will take some time to recap what I've learned. I'll give you a synopsis."

"That will be fine."

"From you, I learned that each component of networking is a system within itself which comprises the total system. I need to be proficient at each component to maximize the benefit of networking.

"From Art, I learned that an infomercial has key components that must be spoken every time an infomercial is given; however, if I meet someone for the first time and they ask what I do, I can give them my benefit statement which is, 'I provide peace of mind for homeowners by protecting one of their most valuable assets.'

"From David Alexander, I learned that when giving a presentation to my networking group I should build the presentation primarily upon how the group can find referrals for me. He emphasized that I was not to spend five minutes explaining how to kill a roach or ant.

"From David Lawler, I learned how to be a referral leader by using a system," finished Clark.

"It sounds like you have absorbed the information very well."

"Words can't describe how excited I am to have you work with me and introduce me to others who have selflessly shared their knowledge with me," Clark proclaimed.

"You are welcome. Since we have a few hours to drive to meet your next educator, why don't you share your background with me."

"It is not very exciting, but I'd be happy to do that. I was born to parents who knew the value of working hard. They were both raised in Georgia, but they moved to California before I was born. We lived there long enough for my sister and me to be born before we returned to Georgia. Since some people think I have an accent, it shocks people when I tell them I was born in a suburb of Los Angeles, California. People tend to think I was born in some place like Texas or Kentucky.

"My Dad was in the Navy near the end of World War II. He had six children from a previous marriage. One thing that amazes me is for all eight of his children a boy would be born, then a girl. You would think that at some point consecutive boys or consecutive girls would have been born, but it did not happen that way. I am the oldest of his younger set of children. From my earliest memories of him, he owned an auto body shop until he became disabled.

"All of my life, he played the guitar and the bass guitar. When I was small, we had a music room where we would record on a reel-to-reel recorder and on an eight-track recorder. Back then there was no such thing as cassette tapes, compact discs or digital recordings. Most music was recorded reel-to-reel and then from there put on records and eventually eight-track tapes.

"He played bass guitar for a country group, Shellcracker and the Drifters. I heard them a few times, and they were fairly decent. Of all his children, only my younger sister and I learned to play music. Shortly after I was born, he was offered $1,000 for his Gibson guitar. He did not accept the offer, and I now have his Gibson guitar. He died in 1987 from cancer."

"I am sorry to hear that," whispered Tim.

"Thanks. Although I am thankful for the good things he put in me, such as a love for music, I was not that close to him. He had a philosophy for life that if someone could do something, he could do it better. I adopted a similar philosophy which states that if someone can do something within reason, I can learn to do it equally well. That's why I am so driven. I want to be the best at everything that I do."

"Clark, from our time together, I've gathered that you are a driven person. When we first met, I picked up on that. I can help people like you who want to succeed but just need some instruction and guidance; however, if someone won't even brush the fly off the end of their nose, it's hard to help them."

"I want to hear some more of your story, but we are within 30 minutes of meeting Gina. I'd like to give you some background information on her."

"That's fine with me," voiced Clark. "If I say too much, not enough or I need to do something differently, please don't hesitate to tell me. You will not hurt my feelings. I want to learn to be a networking guru just like you."

"Clark, I think with your determination, you will surpass me, and that will make me happy. For now, let me give you some information about Gina. She has a fascinating story. She can tell you the details if she desires. Everything that she does, she does it well. Her husband hosts a syndicated home improvement radio show. Through her business, Personal Success Partners, she coaches other business owners to reach higher levels than previously imagined.

"The first time I heard her speak at a meeting, her persona impressed me. When speaking in public, you never know what kind of audience you will have. She stepped to the front of the room and arrested the attention of the entire crowd. Some speakers may woo the audience with something funny or some attention grabber, but then the rest of their speech lacks substance. She had a tremendous amount of substance to her speech.

"Gina has 20 years of corporate experience in sales, customer service and leadership, including 14 years of management, leadership and training experience while she worked for Nordstrom, Inc. She has won numerous awards. She is a founding Board Member of the ChoicePoint Achievement Foundation, a non-profit devoted to developing character and confidence in young people.

"She serves as the South Charlotte Area Networking Director and trainer for 10 local chapters of BNI comprised of over 225 business owners and entrepreneurs."

When they arrived in Charlotte, they met Gina at a famous local restaurant, Mac's Speed Shop.

"Tim, how are you?" asked Gina.

"If I were any better, I'd be Hugh Grey's twin. Gina, how are you?"

"That's phenomenal Tim. Hugh Grey is sensational. The answer to your question is I am fantastic."

"I agree with you about Hugh. I want you to meet Clark," Tim said as he turned to Clark.

"Clark, it is my pleasure to meet you. All I can say is that if Tim has agreed to help you, you have to be a man of high character."

"I do my best."

"Let's order some lunch," suggested Tim.

"Gina, I have been here before, but please tell Clark the best items on the menu."

"Everything on the menu is good, and I've tried most everything. My favorite is the combo platter because I can choose four different kinds of meats. The choices of meats are: hand-pulled pork, beer-can chicken, smoked turkey, St. Louis ribs, Texas beef sausage, and beef brisket. Regardless of your selection of meats, there is something on the platter for everyone."

Clark chimed in, "This sounds like it will be a wonderful dining experience."

Tim recommended ordering a couple of large platters so all of the meat choices could be sampled.

While eating lunch, Gina asked Clark more about his business, and in turn, Clark asked Gina more about her business. When they finished lunch, Tim excused himself and said he would return to pick Clark up in two hours.

"Clark, today we're going to talk about one-to-ones. Regardless of the networking book you read, the networking group you belong to, or the champion networker you meet, they all understand the need for this phase of networking.

"At the typical structured networking meeting, there is time for open networking where you have the opportunity for 10 or 15 minutes to shake hands with a few people and discuss whatever you desire. Then there is time for people to give an infomercial, and at some point in time, one member gives a 7-10 minute presentation. Some networking meetings will allow the presenter to speak before the infomercials, and some will speak after the infomercials.

"What you learn about a member or guest from what you hear at the meeting will be limited. In the length of time that you have at a meeting, you can't learn everything that you need to know about the business or employee of the business. A vehicle designed to help you gain more information about a company or employee from a company commonly goes by the name of one-to-ones.

"Let's discuss some specifics about one-to-ones. The reason for spending the time for one-to-ones is that it gives you the opportunity to learn more about your counterpart so that you can find referrals for him or her. When scheduling one-to-ones, you want to email some basic background information about yourself. Be sure to include marital status, educational background, awards, interests, hobbies and maybe some unique detail about yourself and your company. Have this information typed and saved as a document so that when you schedule your one-to-one, you can email your information to the other person.

"For best results, send an email reminder of the meeting details, along with some personal information, a couple days in advance of your confab. Follow up with a phone call the day before the meeting. The email will read something like this:

> Chad,
>   I hope that all is well. I wanted to remind you that we are scheduled to meet for lunch at noon on Wednesday at Zaxby's on North Broad Street. I look forward to discussing ways we can refer each other. Attached you'll find some basic information about me.
>
> Have a blessed day,
> Gina Herald

"The follow-up phone call would sound similar to the email. 'Chad, this Gina. I hope all is well. I just wanted to confirm our meeting for tomorrow. Did you receive my email and basic information? I will see you tomorrow.'

"When you follow up with an email and also a phone call, it shows you have business acumen. One-to-ones should last approximately one hour. Even though we have so many modern conveniences to save time, it seems as if people are busier now than they have ever been. We don't have time to spend 2-5 hours on one-to-one gatherings. You don't have to meet at a restaurant or coffee shop, but many people do. If that is where you meet, the projected time scheduled for your one-to-one should be 2-3 minutes to extend pleasantries, three minutes to discuss the emailed information sheet, and five minutes to order food or drink. That allows 25 minutes for each of you to talk about your business.

"In a networking group, you will have people who are in similar professions or professions which call on the same kind of clients. People who call on the same kind of clients that you do will be your main referral sources. Some networking aficionados call these groups *contact spheres*.

"There are usually four or five contact spheres in a networking group.

1. Real Estate (sometimes called Home Services)
2. Health & Wellness (sometimes called Medical)
3. Business to Business
4. Financial
5. Marketing & Events

"There are books that explain contact spheres in more detail. For the sake of time, we will deal with your contact sphere.

"The following professions are included in the Real Estate contact sphere: real estate agents, electricians, plumbers, painters, landscapers, pest control companies and cleaning companies. This is not an exhaustive list, but it gives you an idea of the types of businesses that belong in this sphere. Since they deal with the same kind of customers that you do, they are more apt to send referrals your way, and you are more apt to send referrals their way.

"If you are at a customer's home, and you notice that they have paint peeling, you could mention it by saying, 'When I treated the outside of your home, I noticed some paint peeling around the window sills. If not corrected, it can lead to other moisture problems.' Usually they would say thanks and that they noticed it but have not taken care of it. You could say, 'I know a great painter if you need one.'

"While you are there with the customer, it may be hard to open up a conversation about their finances. You wouldn't normally say, 'I finished treating your home. By the way, do you have enough money to retire?' It would be somewhat awkward.

"We discussed contact spheres because statistics have proven that in the arena of networking, 50-75 percent of your referrals will come from your contact sphere. So when you start scheduling your one-to-ones, you want to schedule with those in your contact sphere first. The referral leaders in the chapter are the second group of people with whom it would be the most beneficial to schedule one-to-ones. Did Tim have someone talk to you about referrals yet?"

"Yes. An excellent attorney named David Lawler."

"That's right. Tim told me about that. If in your networking group you have a member or two who passes 10 or more referrals per month, make sure that as soon as you complete one-to-ones with your contact sphere members, you schedule with these referral leaders.

"You should try to schedule 1 one-to-one per week. Tim once told me that when he first started networking with people he had 42 one-to-ones in approximately three months."

"You're kidding me!" Clark responded.

"No." replied Gina. "He is a man who is very driven to succeed. I guess that is the reason many people know him as the networking guru. Like I said, you should try to schedule 1 one-to-one per week, but let me rephrase that. Don't try; just do it! Try is a big failure word and gives people an out. Just set the plan and follow it."

The server stopped by to ask if they needed a refill of their drinks.

At the same time both Gina and Clark replied, "No, but thanks."

Gina stated, "Let's continue. Speaking of a plan, you want to be able to refer your counterpart. When you have a one-to-one, there are some questions you may want to ask.

1. What makes you different from your competition?
2. What area do you service?
3. In your industry, are you price-driven, results-driven, people-driven, superior-service or product-driven?
4. How can I best introduce you or your business to my clients?
5. How long have you been in your industry?
6. What qualifications or certifications do you have?

7. How long have you owned or worked for your current company?

"If you refer the products and services of someone, you really want to know quite a bit of information about them. This is not an exhaustive list, but it is enough to start you on your way. You may add to, subtract from, or tweak the list of questions based upon the profession of your counterpart. Let's look at each question, and I'll explain why you may want to know the answer to them.

1. What makes you different from your competition? Every company needs to have something that sets them apart from the competition. Clark, I will tell you that here in Charlotte there are many pest control companies. If you worked in our region, maybe something different about your company could be that you are willing to work with any schedule. I did some investigation, and most pest control companies only work from 8:00 a.m. to 5:00 p.m. If you go to their home with a smile at 8:00 or 9:00 p.m. (because that is when they make it home from work), that would be something very different about you.

2. What area do you service? If I happen to be in Greensboro and meet someone who needs your service, but you only work in the Charlotte area, that would be important for me to know. I would not want to refer you to an area you don't service.

3. What drives you? If someone does not have the lowest pricing, but the quality far exceeds others or the services are superior to others, that's ok. You just need to know, so when you talk to your clients you can accentuate that point.

4. How can I best introduce you or your business to my clients? A financial planner may be able to give you a question or a statement that wouldn't be offensive to

most people. Correctly using this information can open the door for you to make the introduction.

5. How long have you been in your industry? If you have been in your industry for a few years, that is a good selling point for those referring you to their customers because they can talk about your experience in the industry. If you have been in the industry a short period of time, your referral partners can underscore the positives that you are not stuck in a rut and have fresh new ideas.

6. What qualifications or certifications do you have? Some industries require certifications, while others do not. In reading up on your industry, I found out that there are registered technicians and certified operators. Your manual discusses new technicians having a minimum of 80 hours training before they take their test. Do you only require the minimum, do you go below the minimum or do you exceed it? This is a great selling point because your referral partners can emphasize that your technicians have a minimum of X number of hours of classroom and on the job training. If you have some special qualification, that's really good to know, especially if others in your industry do not trouble themselves to earn that qualification.

7. How long have you owned or worked for your current company? Whether you are new or have been around for a while, your partners can brag on you either way once they know.

"Clark, do you have any questions about what we have discussed so far?"

"Not at this time. Thank you for giving me an explanation of why we want to know this information. I have found that when I do something because it was instructed but I don't understand why, it becomes mechanical, and I become a robot. If I understand why, then my heart is in what I am doing."

"What an excellent way to put it," Gina commented.

"We need to discuss a few more things related to one-to-ones before Tim returns," continued Gina. "My preference when having one-to-ones is to let the other person discuss his or her business first. You don't have to do it that way, but when you do, I think it lets the other person know you're serious about finding them referrals. Hopefully, it will be reciprocated.

"We have people in our area that once they have a one-to-one meeting, they will also set aside a day to ride together to appointments. The merchant services representative and the payroll company, the plumber and the handy man, the painter and the drywall representative, and the financial advisor and the CPA many times call upon the same clients. If one of the referral partners has four to eight appointments scheduled, then they could introduce their counterpart as a trusted business partner.

"The person may already have a relationship with someone who does what your referral partner does. If they do, you can simply say, 'If your current provider fails to meet your expectations, feel free to call on my friend. You could also allow my partner to be on your backup list or use their service if you have an emergency and can't reach your current provider.'

"Clark, there is one more thing I'd like to cover with you before Tim takes you home. Too many times when people attend a mixer or business after hours, they primarily talk to people that they know. Since you are new, you, as well as any other newbies, won't know that many people.

"Although what I am about to tell you is not technically a one-to-one, it could be considered a mini one-to-one. When you approach someone to open a conversation, tell them your name and ask an open-ended question because it requires more than a yes or no answer.

"There are many good questions to ask, but a couple of my favorites are: 'What do you enjoy most about what you do?' and 'Why did you enter the profession in which you are currently employed?' It will allow the person to open up, and you may be able to carry on a 10-minute conversation just based on one of these questions. If it seems that the business relationship should progress, schedule to meet for breakfast or lunch. There are enough piranhas in the World who are out to chew people up; when you make the conversation about the other person, it will be a breath of fresh air to them. They will realize that you are genuine.

"Tim has returned. Clark, are there any questions related to one-to-ones?"

"I don't think so. From my limited knowledge, it sounds as if you covered the topic thoroughly."

"Tim, did you finish all of your errands?" asked Gina.

"I did," Tim replied. "I was able to discuss some business ideas with Hugh Grey. I knew he was an athlete and at one time taught tennis lessons. Did he tell you that he won the tennis championship for his age group this year?"

"No, he did not. Often times he can be modest about his accomplishments."

"After I left his office, I made a few phone calls and responded to some emails."

"Well, we have wrapped up our topic," Gina said.

"I certainly thank you for taking time out of your day to help Clark. Given some time, I believe he will be a networking guru, too," pronounced Tim.

"You're welcome, Tim," stated Gina. "Any time I can be of service, I am willing to do so. Will you be attending the big networking conference in Savannah?"

"Absolutely," Tim said. "I look forward to seeing you there. Clark and I will head toward the home front."

As they drove South, Tim had Clark give him a synopsis of what he learned from Gina.

"She taught me the importance of one-to-ones. In order to pass referrals, I need to learn more about those in my networking groups than what I can find out about them from listening to their infomercials or 7-10 minute presentations. Once I schedule a meeting, I should make sure that I follow up by emailing a reminder and some basic information about myself. She said to schedule one per week. She gave me a list of questions to ask while at the one-to-one meeting.

"Before I forget it, Gina told me that you had 42 one-to-one meetings in approximately three months. I don't want to doubt Gina because she is such a nice young lady, but that seems unreal. Did you really do that?"

"Yes, I did. When I first started learning about networking, I attended a training that lasted approximately three hours. The instructor mentioned that if those attending would schedule at least 1 one-to-one per week, they would be successful. I thought that if one would make you successful, surely an average of three plus per week would make me really successful."

"Tim, I had a gigantic amount of respect for you before today, but I have even more now. What I have learned from the other instructors lets me know that when it comes to networking, you practice what you and other champion networkers preach."

"Clark, growing a network of other professionals around you to fulfill your dreams takes more effort than reading a book or attending a meeting. You don't become a champion networker overnight. You have to implement the entire system to maximize your results. There are plenty of people who can tell you what a book says, but they can't do what the book says, or they have never lived what the book says. Where I am from, we call that being a hypocrite.

"Before we talk some more about what Gina said, I want to tell you an amazing fact that I learned while at a conference," continued Tim. "A few years ago, I attended a conference in Tulsa, and one of the speakers told the audience that to be considered an expert one must put at least 10,000 hours of study into their area of expertise. We live in a society where many people do not want to work for what they obtain, or if they do work, they want to do the bare minimum.

"Too many people have what I call 'the drive thru window mentality' when it comes to life. When I was growing up, it was common for families to eat the evening meal together, but now it's so much easier for a family to go to the drive thru window at their favorite fast food restaurant. In most households today, both the Dad and the Mom work just to make ends meet.

"Let me learn quickly because I don't want it taking too long. Clark, I don't know about you, but I was not born with a silver spoon in my mouth. I have had to work for what my wife and I have. I like what your Daddy said that if someone else could do a job, then he could learn to do it better. If I had been born into a family with wealth, I might not have learned to appreciate things like I do. Well, that's enough on that. Let's talk some more about what Gina taught you."

"She told me to schedule one-to-ones with those business professionals closely related to mine and then to schedule them with the networking referral leaders. In the Charlotte area, she said that some networking members after they have a meeting, will schedule a day where they will ride together on appointments to introduce their referral partner to a potential client.

"Clark, it sounds like she covered the topic well."

"She did."

"Now, tell me some more about your background. You told me about your Dad, but I would like to hear about your Mom."

"My Mother was a good country girl who loved people. Although we live in an ever-changing society, some things remain the same. In recreational softball at Church, school or some other event, if two captains choose the individuals who make up their respective teams, the girls are always picked last. In the case of my Mama, they would pick a couple of boys, but she was usually picked third to sixth overall. She could flat out hit a softball. She played guitar and sang. She taught my sister and me to love God and love people. She also taught us to help others, and she lived her life as an example for us to follow.

"My Mama and Dad separated and later divorced when I was seven. I didn't like that at all. It seemed like all the other children at school had both a Mom and a Dad at home. It shook my world. For approximately eight years, my Mama raised us by herself. While we were at school, she would work. Shortly after the school bus carried us home, she would come home from work. Most nights we would eat supper together. She gave her life unconditionally for us.

"From the third grade through the fifth grade, we attended two different schools each year because we moved so much. Finally, when I went to the sixth grade, we stayed in the same school for the entire year. This thrilled me because I was finally able to start building friendships, we moved again; but we were able to attend the same school for two consecutive years.

"The school that we attended does not even exist anymore, but at that time, there were a few elementary schools in the County. Chester, which is where we attended, Chauncey, Rhine, Dodge Elementary and Dodge Middle are the schools I remember. I am bringing this up because during football season the elementary schools would play against each other on Saturday mornings.

"Even though I had never played any kind of organized sports, I tried out and made the football team. Since it was all new to me and I didn't understand what I was doing, I was given one of the last uniforms, which was way too big. In one particular game at the start of the season, we were playing against Chauncey. The running back from Chauncey ran around the left end. I probably could have caught him but my pants were so large that I was chasing him while holding up my pants with both hands. Tim, I wish you could have seen that debacle. It looked like something from a comedy of errors."

Clark continued telling Tim about his Mother and his childhood as they drove toward Georgia.

"Clark, you have an amazing story, and I want to hear more but we've almost made it back to your car. Let's meet at Curt's again tomorrow morning at 9:30 a.m."

"Sounds good. I will see you then."

CHAPTER 7

Giving to Others

On Thursday, Tim and Clark met at Curt's as planned.

"How are you today?" asked Tim.

"Extremely blessed. How about you?"

"If I were any better, I'd be twins. Instead of eating our normal breakfast here at Curt's, we're going to meet your next educator for lunch. It's an hour and a half from here. We can take my car."

Tim's car was comfortable and immaculate. During the drive, Tim told Clark to share some more of his story.

"Are you sure, Tim? My story is not some award-winning novel, and I sure don't want to bore you with it."

"Clark, what I have heard so far astounds me and will amaze others. You need to tell your story and keep telling it. One day you will be a networking guru, and it benefits others to know that people can come from humble beginnings, achieve great things in life, and remain humble.

"I know of a man who drives a 1992 Silverado truck that has one door so rusted that it stays closed with duct tape; the truck bed also has more rust than the door. If you saw the man, you would think he's barely making it, but he has more wealth than most realize. His family lives with him in a fine 11,000 square-foot house. People need to know how real people succeed, as opposed to what Hollywood depicts in its films. I'm really interested in hearing more of your story."

"Ok," replied Clark. "Do you know where I left off?"

"Yes. You were playing football and chasing a guy while holding up your oversized pants."

"That's right," voiced Clark. "After the seventh grade football year, my Mama watched a television special about high school and college football players being paralyzed. She said it was a sign from God, and I could not play football any more. In the eighth grade, I was going to be a starting player, not just a part-time player. She didn't know that we practiced during school. Although I practiced football during school, I could not make it to the games without her driving me.

"The coach came to our house and tried to persuade her to let me play, but she refused.

"A small cluster of students at our little school received allowances for chores like taking out the trash or making their beds. In our family, everyone pitched in and did what was needed. I learned about hard work and sacrifice early in life.

"Let me back up a little bit. At the time, I didn't think about it because it was just our life. We were very poor. I took out the trash, made my bed, washed dishes, learned to cook or do anything else that was needed. If I didn't, there was no such thing as 'time out' for punishment. The only 'time out' that we had was to take time out to go cut our own switch for punishment, and it had better be the right size. My Mama had a way of making that switch work on my rear quarters, and I learned how to dance very well.

"Occasionally, Mama would say, 'This is going to hurt me worse than it's going to hurt you.' I felt like saying, 'Well, because I love you so much, I don't want you to hurt that bad, so let's change places.'

"Since I didn't have an allowance and because we had no extra money, when I participated in a school activity that required new shoes, new clothes or some kind of participation fee, I had to pay for these items myself.

"In the community where I grew up, there was a man who owned fields of squash. When the squash were ready to be harvested, he would pay several of us to pick his squash. We would pick a five-gallon bucket of squash, and when the bucket was emptied on the truck, a quarter would be put into the empty bucket. I started working for him when I was 11 years old and worked for him about three years. I later planted and hoed squash and worked with his hogs. When I did anything for him other than pick squash, I was paid by the hour. I started out at $1.00 per hour, but by time I finished working for him, I was making $1.50 per hour. I thought I had arrived. I was 14 years old and making $1.50 per hour.

"I also worked for our landlord. He had several different fields, and he would pay us $1.00 per hour to pull big weeds out of his fields. In the Summer, I would work 12-14 hours a day because I made more money. I never considered taking a day off because I was tired."

"It seems like we have similar backgrounds because we grew up poor as well," interjected Tim.

"My sister and I grew up playing musical instruments and singing. My sister is one of the most-talented people I know. Give her any length of time with a musical instrument, and she will figure out how to play it.

"When I was 12, my family played and sang at the local fair, and a group that traveled with Waylon Jennings also performed. They heard me play the bass guitar and asked if I wanted to play in their group."

"Clark, if I have this correct, you sing, play musical instruments, play sports and kill bugs. Is there anything you can't do?"

"I can't sew."

Both men laughed.

"When David Lawler showed us his vintage bass guitar, you never said that you played. Why? Did you not like his bass guitar?"

"The reason I didn't mention that I play is because I didn't want to get sidetracked discussing music. I want to learn this system. I did like the look and sound of his new bass guitar."

"I understand. I'm sorry that I interrupted you. Please continue with your story."

"When we grew up, we learned to do many things. My Mama remarried when I was about 15. She married a man who really loved her. Although many times I wished that my Mom and Dad had remarried, my Stepdad was a good man," finished Clark.

"I hate to cut your story short since I am thoroughly enjoying it, but we are close to the restaurant where we will meet your next educator."

"Tim, that's perfectly fine."

"Let me share with you some of his background information," stated Tim. "We can pick up at this point of your story on the way back home."

"Sounds good to me."

"Derek is a brilliant young man," announced Tim. "He graduated from high school at 16 and from college at 20. He and his wife have three children. He worked mainly in IT (computers) before starting his current business, Pop-N-Go, with his partner. They repair the screens of broken or cracked smart phones, tablets and iPads. They can repair them cheaper than most people's deductible and are very successful.

"Because Derek understands the concepts of networking, he would be successful if he were a street sweeper."

After they arrived at the Top Spice Restaurant, Tim asked Derek about the status of his business and his family.

"The business is up 44 percent since the first of the year," declared Derek.

"I am happy for you," remarked Tim.

"My wife and children are doing well."

"Clark, this is my good friend, Derek."

"Derek, it is good to meet you," acknowledged Clark.

"Likewise to you," said Derek.

"Derek, I need to run some errands, so I'll leave Clark with you. I will return in a couple of hours."

"What if I become long-winded, and I am not finished," asked Derek.

"You take your time. If you're not finished when I come back, I will wait."

"Tim, you know I'm just pulling your leg. Before you leave, will you ask your wife to send me the recipes for the grape salad, the hash brown casserole and the butterscotch dessert that we had when we had the cookout at your home? Your wife can cook, and the steaks, fish and chicken that you grilled were some of the best that I have ever eaten in my life."

"I am glad that you enjoyed my contributions to the meal. You are correct. My wife can cook. I will call her when I leave and ask her to email you those recipes."

Tim left with a wave. The other two settled down at a quiet table.

"Derek, what's good to eat here?" asked Clark.

"They have the best fried rice and any kind of meat with it just tops it off. I have tried all of it."

"I'll try the fried rice with shrimp," Clark decided.

"You will love that choice."

While they waited for their food, Derek said, "Tim tells me you have been in the pest control industry for several years."

"That's right. I started with a large nationally known company. They had good training programs, and I worked hard to learn everything there is to know about how to treat pests and termites. When I started my own company, I thought people would do business with me because I am good at what I do. That didn't happen. Everything I'm learning from Tim and the other mentors should make things much better before long."

"Today, I want to instruct you on the giving back portion of networking. Regardless of what type of networking group you belong to, there are consistent ways to give back to the members of the group. In service-oriented groups and casual-contact or open-networking groups, there may not be a place on the agenda of the meeting to give back, but in most closed networking groups, it's built into the agenda.

"Let's talk about closed networking groups first. Most of the time, they have an agenda where everyone has the opportunity to give an infomercial. Some groups will allow one member each week to give a 7-10 minute presentation; others will allow for two members to give shorter presentations. It works best to have only one member give a longer presentation. In a few minutes, the reason for this will be evident."

"Derek, would the reason for preferring one presenter versus two be that the meeting lasts longer with two presenters?"

"Since you asked that question, I know that you are thinking about the process. That's not the reason, but here's what happens when they have two speakers versus one. Most closed networking meetings last an hour to an hour and a half.

"When a group chooses to have one spotlight speaker, the other members usually have 45-60 seconds for their infomercial. If a group allows two speakers, the infomercial time may only be 30 seconds; however, the overall length of the meeting does not change.

"Toward the end of the meeting, the members have a chance to give back to the group. The infomercial is all about the member or the member's company and the spotlight speaker's presentation is all about him or her in detail.

"The portion at the end is no longer about the member, but it's about another member. When groups operate this portion of the meeting correctly, it becomes a thing of beauty.

"Three ways exist where a member can give back during this portion of the meeting. A member can bring guests. This shows he or she is giving back to the entire group because the guest(s) can potentially do business with other members of the group, or if their classification is open, they could apply for membership.

"Another way to give back is by passing referrals to other members of the group. If my information is correct, David Lawler talked to you about referrals, and he showed you a method where you can average several referrals per month."

"He showed me a system that he uses, and I plan on being another Jamie," avowed Clark.

"Are you talking about Jamie who lives in North Carolina?" asked Derek.

"Yes. David said that she averages 25-35 referrals per month."

"I know her, and that is correct. What an awesome example of selfless giving."

The two paused a moment when the waiter brought their food.

"If you use the system that David showed you and you have several referrals that you passed in a week, you'll want to stand and tell everyone how many referrals you gave in the past week but only highlight one of them.

"The third way that you can give back is by giving a testimonial about another member. If you give a testimonial, it works when you state the testimonial, but works even better when you also have it in writing on your company's letterhead so you can give it to the member.

"When you bring a guest, pass referrals or give a testimonial, only talk about one of the three. I am going to make a statement that everyone who networks needs to learn and understand. Light that is focused can do surgery. When a member attends a meeting and talks about passing a referral to Clint, one to Sally and one to Luke, there is no focused spotlight. The light becomes weak and dissipated. If, however, a member says, 'I passed three referrals, but I want to talk about the referral for Clint.' the light stays focused on Clint," Derek explained.

"Is this the reason you prefer one spotlight speaker as opposed to two?" asked Clark.

"That is the exact reason," Derek answered. "Most phenomenal networking groups will have a constant influx of guests. If you have two speakers, do the guests focus on speaker one or speaker two? What if both speakers are equally good at what they do, but one happens to be a more polished presenter or has more charisma than the other? The other speaker looks like he or she doesn't know his or her business, even if they know it better than the other speaker."

"I totally understand," Clark responded.

"Let me give you an example of how you would give each of these.

"Let's just say you brought three guests, but only one is eligible to submit an application because that classification is open. You can say, 'I have three guests today, and one is interested in becoming part of our team.' If you have more than one guest who is eligible to submit an application, then maybe you say, 'I have guests today who are interested in our group.' You can also just say, 'I have three guests today.' and leave it at that.

"Let me give you an example of referrals being passed. The referrals are usually passed during the week leading up to the meeting, but they are discussed at the meeting. Example: 'I passed five referrals this past week. I want to talk about the one I passed to Sally. We had a customer whose AC unit was not cooling very well and didn't know who to call. While we were at the customer's home, we called Sally's company. A representative came out on the same day. Our customer loves them, and says because of her company, they are cool now.'

"The last example will be for giving a testimonial. Example: 'I have a testimonial for Luke. We have a customer who went to the large local car dealership to have a problem diagnosed. They told her it would cost $2,300 to repair the problem. I told her about Luke, a local man, who owns a shop that is a good alternative to the higher-priced dealership. After Luke's people looked at the problem, they repaired it for $459. Our customer thanked me for referring her to Luke, and she has been referring her friends.'

"Clark, some people don't understand conjunctions very well. They think that the conjunctions *and* and *or* mean the same thing, but they don't. Clark, discuss referrals or guests or a testimonial, but not referrals and guests and a testimonial. Does this make sense?"

"Yes. I believe you are telling me to focus on only one of the three choices and not two or three of the three choices," replied Clark.

"You've got it. So far, have you heard me say, 'I want to report closed business?'"

"No," answered Clark.

"You know why?" Derek asked.

"Not really," answered Clark. "I would think you would want people to know that you are reporting closed business from a referral."

"Remember, Clark," continued Derek. "This portion of the meeting is not about you anymore. If you want to talk about closed business, then tie it into your infomercial. Closed business is all about you. Did you hear me say, 'I want to thank Sally for referring Chris to me?'"

"No," said Clark thoughtfully.

"That is also about me. I would not be thanking her if she had not given to me. Did you hear me say, 'I met with Henry for a one-to-one?'"

"No," Clark replied.

"Do you know why?" asked Derek.

"I don't," answered Clark. "I would think you would want to let everyone know that you are scheduling one-to-ones with members outside of the normal meeting. You want to show them you are trying."

"Clark, do you understand the purpose of one-to-one meetings?" asked Derek.

"I get it now," Clark said nodding his head. "One-to-one meetings are held to find out more about a fellow member so that you can find him or her referrals. So if you mentioned I met Henry for a one-to-one, then that makes it all about you."

"Did I mention saying, 'I don't have anything today?'"

"No."

"That's because you should have a guest, a referral or a testimonial at every meeting you attend. Did I mention telling the spotlight speaker, 'That was a great presentation today'? By saying that, you contributed absolutely nothing.

"While I am talking about this part, once upon a time I visited a networking group. The owner was the member. He could not attend the meeting so he called one of his technicians about two hours before the scheduled start time and told him to go to the meeting. He called him again one hour before the meeting started and said, 'By the way, you have to give the 10-minute presentation today.' The man was probably an outstanding technician, but he definitely needed to work on his speaking skills.

"When he first started speaking he said, 'Now, I ain't no speaker.' If anyone has ever told the truth, he told the truth that day. For approximately nine minutes of his 10-minute presentation, he would look at a picture, laugh about it and say, 'This is a job we did one time; y'all look at this.' It was the worst presentation I had ever heard. It made his company look like a bunch of bumbling nincompoops. At the end of the meeting, at least half of the chapter members stood and said, 'That was a great presentation.' I felt like standing and telling them they were all liars.

"Did I mention that my boy is playing soccer, and we are raising money or that my girl is selling Girl Scout cookies if anyone wants to purchase a box?"

"No."

"Clark, you must understand this section of the meeting focuses on others. Champion networkers understand this well. The average person who attends networking meetings does not grasp this concept.

"Now let's look at how you can give back to those of a service-oriented or casual-contact group. Most of the time, they do not have a format where referrals or testimonials are openly discussed like they have at a closed networking group. Although one can, and should, pass referrals, the format of the meeting does not allow you to talk about the referrals that have been passed. What I'm about to explain needs to be done before the meeting or after the meeting. Another way to give back besides passing referrals is to have a networking friend attend the meeting and give a brief testimonial about that individual.

"Let me give you an example of this. Let's just say your friend has a landscaping business. At the meeting, you walk up to the Realtor and say, 'Hello, John, I hope all is well. I'd like to introduce you to Joe. He owns Perfect Earth Landscaping. They work primarily in the north end of the County for regular maintenance but work in the surrounding Counties for installs. This man's company does some outstanding work. They are the best landscaping company in our area.' Give your buddy a few minutes to talk with the person, and then you can come back together. He or she can then introduce you to someone.

"Most after-hours events generally have refreshments and gear the meeting toward walking around and talking to different people. Often, these events will have a larger attendance than a normal networking meeting. I have seen as many as 500 people at an after-hours event. You still want to go to these with a buddy. Your goal is not to talk to all 500 people, just a few key people who could become referral partners with you. Most after-hours events will last one and a half to two hours.

"In advance, ask your buddy who some key contacts for him or her would be. At the event, introduce your buddy to the desired business professional and give a brief testimonial as part of the introduction. Allow a few minutes for them to talk, and then meet up again. Your buddy can then introduce you to a key contact. If you both manage to make two or three good connections, you have had a successful night. Each of you must follow up with your connections.

"The old saying holds true, 'The money is in the follow-up.' Go to each meeting with a plan. Don't go to hang out or talk about things that really don't matter in the scope of life. Getting sidetracked by discussing family, politics, sports or the economy remains a pitfall for the novice networker. I'm not saying you can't mention these things, but don't spend half of the meeting time discussing sports. Clark, am I clear on this point?"

"Yes, Sir. I understand you loud and clear."

"Tim, I see you made it back," remarked Derek.

"Absolutely, Derek. How did things go?"

"I was just about to recap what we've discussed," Derek stated.

"Ok. I'll wait in the car. I need to respond to some messages. Before I go though, I just spoke with Austin Bartos. He owns a local cell phone store that also sells tablets. I asked him if anyone ever brought in a phone with a cracked screen.

"He said, 'Yes.'

"I asked him what he did when folks came in with a cracked screen. He said, 'If the device is still under warranty, I tell clients to file a claim. If the device is out of warranty, I tell the clients about new devices.' I discussed you and your company, and he said that he would be interested in meeting with you. Here's his card."

"Tim, thank you. You are definitely the networking guru."

"Thanks for the kind words, but I was just looking out for my friend," Tim replied.

He waved his hand as he walked outside.

"To recap what we've discussed, I will let you tell me about giving to others in regards to various networking events. I have found that when it comes to learning, if you can at least give a synopsis of what you have been taught, then you are well on your way to being able to apply the principles."

"I will do my best," Clark responded. "I'm sure that I will not be able do justice to what you have taught me, but I'll do my best.

"In a closed networking meeting, such as BNI, the infomercial time is all about the member and the spotlight presentation is about the member in more detail. The portion at the end is about giving back. It is no longer about that particular member."

"So far your recall has been excellent," noted Derek.

"During the giving back portion at the end of the meeting, there are three legitimate choices a member has available to properly demonstrate the previous week's activities:

1. The number of referrals but only discuss details of one;
2. Only one testimonial; or

3. Introduce your guest(s)

"Clark, remember you can do surgery with light that is focused. That is the reason for only talking in detail about one of three things."

"I do remember you saying that. Thanks for the reminder."

"Please continue with your synopsis, Clark."

"You also said that a member should only state one of the three available options, not all three."

"In a service-oriented group or open-networking group, introduce a buddy to others who could benefit him or her and give a short testimonial. Referrals work as well, but the format of the meeting does not usually allow for the discussion of any giving back. The introduction of a buddy has to be before or after the meeting, but if it is an after-hours function, it can be throughout the time frame of the meeting."

"Clark, it sounds to me like you have the information in your head, but my hope is that it goes all the way to the core of your being and becomes part of who you are. Here comes our waiter."

Derek asked for the check.

"The bill has already been paid replied the waiter."

"Clark, I'll bet Tim paid for our food either before he left or when he came back. He truly embraces a philosophy that it is more blessed to give than receive."

When they reached the car, Derek said goodbye to Clark and Tim.

Clark shook his hand and said, "Thanks again, Derek, for helping me with this portion of networking."

"You look excited, Clark," Tim said.

"I am. I have learned so much over the past few days. I am chomping at the bit to put it to practice. Thanks for lunch," Clark added.

"Glad to do it. We have one more person to give you instruction, and then you can put all of this training into practice."

"I can hardly wait. Tim, I have learned so many aspects of networking for which I am grateful, but I have a question."

"Go right ahead and ask your question."

"Derek really opened my understanding of some key actions to take in networking groups. He spoke briefly about bringing guests. How do you find guests to bring to the meetings?

"If I am involved with the three main types of networking groups, a service organization, an open and a closed group and they work well for me, wouldn't I want to invite others to be part of these groups?"

"Clark, some people might say no because their desire stems from wanting to shut others out and hoard as much business as they can for themselves, but champion networkers want to invite as many business owners or representatives of businesses as possible to at least evaluate a meeting to determine if the concept would work for them.

"The answer to your question is yes, and your educator scheduled for tomorrow will teach you all about the art of inviting.

"Fantastic!" exclaimed Clark.

"Now, tell me more about your history," Tim said.

"Did I leave off with my Mama marrying a wonderful man when I was 15?" Clark asked.

"Yes."

"Mama didn't allow me to play football any more, but I was a point guard on our basketball team in high school. Most people will tell you someone 5'7" should not be able to jump, but I could touch the rim. I was the exception to the rule. At the same time, I was playing the bass guitar for a music group that traveled on weekends. It was time for summer basketball camp, and even though I had raised the money to go to camp, it was going to conflict with the travel schedule of the music group. I really wanted to do both, but it was going to be impossible. When my Stepdad gave me an ultimatum to either play for the musical group or play basketball, I quit the basketball team and the group.

"The next three years were kind of a blur until I enlisted in the Navy. At age 16, I worked at a new grocery store chain. They allowed me to work 20-30 hours per week in the beginning, but because of the overstaffing for the grand opening, one week they cut my hours to four. I thought about quitting, but I decided not to. My hours picked up, and even though I was in high school, I worked 72 hours in one particular week and never missed school. The more I worked, the more I made.

"When I turned 16, I saved up $200 and borrowed $50 to buy an older-model car. That car had a four-barrel carburetor and drank quite a bit of gas. I drove it for a few months, but my folks had an old Datsun pickup that they said they would sell me. All I had to do was take over the payments. I was so excited. That truck would only run 60 miles per hour downhill with a tornado behind it. It didn't bother me because I spent half the amount of money on gas.

"I remember during this time period in my life that some young people would peel out and burn rubber, others on Friday night would drive through a certain area over and over (driving the strip). Those young people didn't have to pay for their gas or tires, but I did, so I never did those things nor did I ever desire to do those things.

"Just before deciding to join the military, I left the grocery store and went to work in a fast food restaurant. The manager's wife and I had worked together at the grocery store so he knew me and knew I had good work habits. I worked there for a few months before going to boot camp. I enjoyed my time there. I loved it when they would run the quarter pounder special because I would devour four quarter pounders with the fries and a drink.

"I went to see the Navy recruiter because my Dad and oldest half-brother were also in the Navy. When I took the ASVAB test, I qualified for any program that I wanted except the nuclear program. I thought I wanted to be an airplane mechanic but I wasn't 100 percent sure. The recruiter said I could go in as a non-designated striker which meant I would go to boot camp and apprentice training school, and then figure it out later. I signed the dotted line for this option. After attending boot camp in Orlando and delving into a four-week apprentice training program, I was supposed to go to an aircraft carrier.

"While we were in the second week of the apprentice training, an E-5 came into our classroom and told us of different programs that were available. When he mentioned the submariner program, a friend of mine asked if there was any extra pay. The man replied, 'Yes. They have approximately $100 per month sea pay and $100 per month sub pay.' Since I was an E-1 and was making very little money, I signed up immediately. I later found out that you don't receive sea pay until you make E-4, and sub pay was only $50 per month.

"Mama didn't put up with any junk when we grew up. Her discipline prepared me for my military journey. Do you mind if I tell you a couple of funny stories that happened in boot camp?"

"Please do. I am enjoying learning more about your background," Tim stated.

"In the Navy, we had company commanders who are comparable to drill sergeants in the other branches of the service. We were issued five pairs of pants, shirts, tee shirts, underwear and socks. They didn't want us to rotate wearing just two pairs of pants and shirts so we could leave the rest folded in our lockers. They wanted us to constantly fold the clothes in our lockers.

"One young man thought he could fool the company commanders by not rotating through his clothes. He didn't want to have to fold the clothes in his locker every day. On one occasion, the company commanders made us all stand at attention for a locker inspection. When they noticed that this young man had some new clothes that had not been washed, they told him to go get a bucket of water, and he was going to wash the clothes by hand. He had to send them through the wash cycle, the rinse cycle and the spin cycle. While he was washing his clothes, he had to keep repeating the following:

'Rub, dub, dub, I'm a Maytag washing machine. I wash all day, and I wash all night, and my parts never break down.'"

"Clark, are you kidding me?"

"Tim, I'm for real."

"Well, if I had been there, I would have been in trouble because I would have laughed the entire time he was saying that," Tim laughed.

"Several of us did start laughing. By time the company commander turned around, all of us had stopped. He made a few of us drop and give him 25 pushups. I had completed 20 when he asked me how many I had done, to which I replied, '20, Sir.'

"He said, 'Recruit, I have not heard you count any.' I had to start over and after each push up say the number and sir."

"So you ended up doing 45, instead of 25?"

"That is correct."

"Wow!"

"Because I was in good shape, it didn't bother me." After pausing for a couple of minutes, Clark began the next story.

"We had a few men who snored when they slept. Two young men in our company thought it would be funny to put shaving cream in the mouths of those who snored. The company commanders somehow found out about this incident, and they made the entire company stand at attention. One of the company commanders started to rant and rave.

"He said, 'I want to know who did this. You better step forward because if you don't, you are going to be in serious trouble.'

"The two young men eventually stepped out. The company commander had both of them hold out their arms, with their palms up. He put shaving cream in each hand and told them to stand there. After about a minute, one young man's hands dropped a little bit, and some shaving cream fell on the floor.

"When the company commander saw this, he got face to face with the young man and shouted, 'Recruit, if you drop any more shaving cream on my floor, you are going to eat it!'

"A couple more minutes passed, and his hands dropped a little more and some shaving cream fell on the floor. The company commander got in his face and hollered, 'Eat it, eat it, eat it!' and the recruit shoved it all in his mouth."

"It sounds as if you had quite the experience in boot camp."

"It was a blast."

"I definitely want to hear more, but we are back at your car," Tim told him.

"I didn't mean to talk your ears off. I was engrossed in reliving the past, and I lost sight of where we were."

"You didn't talk my ears off," replied Tim. "I like to know a person's background. When working with people, it helps to know their background. It gives teachers insight as to why students make certain decisions or behave a certain way. Regardless of how self-sufficient a person may be, everyone needs help from time to time. Listen to me; if you see a turtle on a fence post, you know it did not get there by itself. Some people think that they are self-made, but no one is self-made. We all come into this world owing nine month's room and board.

"Let's meet again in the morning at Curt's at 9:00 a.m. Our next educator has some appointments in the area after 1:00 p.m. She has agreed to come over early so she can teach you the final topic of this training program. She will be here at 9:15 a.m., but we still need to meet at 9 a.m. so I can tell you more about her."

"I'll be here."

CHAPTER 8

Inviting to Grow Your Network

"Hello, Clark. Are you ready to eat a good breakfast so you can learn the last aspect of networking?"

"Yes," answered Clark.

"Better yet, why don't we wait until your next educator arrives, and we can eat breakfast together," suggested Tim.

"I like that idea even better," proclaimed Clark.

"In the meantime, let me tell you about her. Cathy Barbieri owns a carpet cleaning business. She is married to a wonderful man, and they have three children. She began her venture in networking 19 years ago. When it comes to inviting people to a meeting, she definitely has the inviting mindset. For many years, she has been a BNI Senior Director. She's forgotten more about networking than most will ever know. A man who was in a chapter with her told me she continually brought guests and referrals to the meeting. Here she is now."

After Tim and Cathy hugged, he told her "I want you to meet my friend, Clark."

"It's good to meet you, Clark," Cathy said.

"I feel the same way, Cathy. Tim has told me so much about you."

Tim chimed in, "Cathy, we waited on you to eat. I'm starving so let's go through the line, and you can order something from the menu or make a plate from the buffet."

"I just want biscuits, gravy and coffee," replied Cathy.

"I think I will order two eggs over medium, hash browns, country ham, toast and orange juice," declared Tim thoughtfully. "What'll you have, Clark?"

"Tim, I'll have the same as you."

While they ate their breakfast, Tim asked Cathy about the status of her business and about her family.

"Mike and the children are doing well," she decreed. "The carpet cleaning business has grown 20 percent over the last year."

"Outstanding!" Tim responded.

After they ate their breakfast, Tim announced, "I'm going to leave you two. I'll be back in a couple of hours. Don't feel like you have to rush, because I come here all the time, and they don't mind us occupying a table to discuss business."

"Ok, Tim," replied Cathy. "We'll see you later."

"Clark, I am here to discuss inviting people to the networking meetings that you attend. We'll discuss a copious amount of information, including proven ways to invite and how I personally invite. If you apply yourself, the different aspects of networking will become part of you. Inviting people to networking events must become a mindset. It should be focused and with intent.

"Whom you invite to a meeting depends on the type of group and your purpose. You must understand the overall scope of inviting.

"I may say some things that appear to be contradictory if you compared one statement versus another, but when you look at the total picture, they blend together.

"From time to time, a service-oriented group or casual-contact group, such as a Chamber of Commerce, will have an attendance drive. When they do, the purpose is to invite anyone and everyone to become a member. Some of these groups will have trips or other prizes based upon the number of sold memberships or sponsorship dollars raised.

"I want to be clear on a point right now. Don't ever invite someone to a meeting with the thought in mind that if you can talk a few people into signing up you can win a trip to Aruba. A trip to Aruba might be nice, but that is not the right reason for inviting them to your meeting. When inviting people to attend a meeting, you want to expose them to the group, and if they see some benefit, then have them apply for membership. Since there can be multiple people of every profession in these types of meetings, you can always invite someone, but I want you to realize that once a year they have a big push for new members.

"If you belong to a closed networking group, the main purpose of inviting is to increase the size of the chapter since they only allow one member per profession. You can ask different members of your group which professions are not currently in the chapter, but they would like to have an introduction to. Then look to invite those people.

"We could have seven different business professionals to whom the group members would like to have an introduction. You can take one profession per week and work on inviting that profession. Instead of inviting everyone, you will focus on one of the desired professions per week.

"There are approximately 30 different ways to identify a specific person to invite. If we discussed all of them, we would be here for the rest of the day, so we will talk about a few of them. Let's suppose we are looking to invite a plumber.

1. Phone conversations – When we are finishing any phone conversation we have, we ask 'Do you know a plumber who works in XYZ area?' If they do, then write down the information so you can contact them. We will talk about the dialogue when we finish the identifying portion.
2. Social Media – Ask the same question to all of your friends and any groups that you belong to.

"For these first two ways, if someone tells you about a plumber, then you ask him or her if they could introduce you by email. Most of the time they will not have the email address of their plumber, so ask, 'Do I have permission to use your name when I talk to him or her?"'

3. Vehicle Signage – Plumbers often have signage on their vehicles. When you see their vehicle graphics, write down their information.
4. Support Team – Call, text or email family, friends, neighbors and co-workers and ask them if they know a plumber who works in XYZ area.
5. Bulletin Boards – Some restaurants and other commercial establishments will have bulletin boards where business professionals can leave their business cards.

"Clark, are you with me so far?"
"Yes, I believe so."
"There are four main vehicles that are used to invite.

1. Electronic media – emails, texts and social media; the main way is email
2. Regular Mail
3. Phone Calls
4. Face to Face

"Clark, of these four different vehicles or avenues of inviting someone to a meeting, how would you rank them in order of effectiveness, with one being the most effective and four being the least effective?"

"Since we are in the technology age, I'd say number one would be email, and I don't have a clue about the order of the others. Different thoughts about each of them keep rolling around in my head. I could see where face to face could be effective because you can see people's reaction and respond to them, but then people are so busy. Who has time to stop and talk these days? I can see where a phone call could be effective. Most of the calls I receive are from telemarketers, and I know how I hate to talk to them. Regular mail could be good because it would not take up as much time as a phone call, but that's old-fashioned. Now I'm not against old-fashioned; I just don't see how effective it would be. Considering I have told you about each of them, I think I can rank them in order of effectiveness.

1. Email
2. Face to Face
3. Regular mail
4. Phone call

"Clark, I am glad to see that you put some thought into your answers. I will give you the order and the explanation for the order. I found out a long time ago that for many people if they know a rule, but don't understand the purpose for the rule, they never embrace the rule; however, if they know the why, then they are more apt to embrace it. It does not mean that they have to absolutely love the rule, but at least it lends credence to the rule.

"Since networking is about relationships and forming meaningful relationships, people have to be personable; it stands to reason then that inviting would have to be personable. So the following are ranked by the most personable to the least personable."

1. Face to face – When you meet with someone face to face, it's easier to read the emotions, read the eyes and observe more about the person you are inviting. You can ask questions and answer questions that the person may have regarding the group to which you are inviting him or her. You also are able to see how busy the person is and take note whether another time would be better for your invitation.

2. Phone call – Everything related to face to face applies to inviting via a phone call, except being able to see how busy they are. You can hear emotion and inflection in their voice. You can have some dialogue.

3. Regular mail – If people receive something from you on your letterhead, they are more apt to read it than an email. Since people receive many pieces of junk mail, it's best to write your company's address and their address as opposed to have it pre-printed on the envelope. It will set your letter apart from the junk mail. You can't read, hear or see any emotions or answer any questions. Write your letter in a way that it interests them, and they will call or show up at the meeting.

4. Email – This is the least time-consuming way of reaching out to people, and people know it. It is, however, a great way to follow up with invitees. When a person uses Constant Contact, it takes very little time to email several people at once.

"There are different schools of thought on the actual conversation that should take place when inviting. We will talk about three proven ways. Regardless of which way you choose, just perfect it and use it on a regular basis. The ways that we will discuss work for inviting in person and when you have a phone conversation with an invitee. When you only have a phone conversation, early in the conversation you want to identify yourself and who referred you to him or her. The conversations that we'll discuss have to be adjusted slightly based upon a phone conversation or a face-to-face conversation. In a few minutes, I will give you a sample of a letter that you can mail or email.

Grip

This is an acronym where each letter stands for part of the process.

G – Grow
R – Referrals
I – Invitation
P – Place and time

"The conversation goes like this: 'Joseph, are you looking to **Grow** your business?'
'Yes.'
'Are **Referrals** important to you?'
'Yes.'
'I would like to **Invite** you to meet some of my business partners who are looking to refer business to someone like you. The **Place** we meet is the 1818 Club on Sugarloaf, and the **Time** we meet is 8:30 a.m. on Wednesdays. I will gladly introduce you to your new business partners.'"

ABC's of Inviting

This is also an acronym where each letter stands for part of the process.

A – Ask
B – By Referrals
C - Commit

"The conversation goes like this: 'Joseph, **are you looking to grow your business <u>by referrals</u>**?'
'Yes.'
'Would you **commit** to meeting a group of business partners who are looking to refer business to someone like you?'

Memorized Script

'Hello, Joseph. The reason for my call is that from time to time clients in my industry need someone who does what you do. I don't have anyone that I refer to on a regular basis, and I'd like to get to know you and your staff better for the possibility of referring clients to you. Would you like to get together?'

'Sure.'

'At 8:30 a.m. on Wednesday, I will be attending a meeting at the 1818 Club on Sugarloaf. Why don't you bring some of your business cards, and we can talk for a little while after the meeting. I will email introduce you to my referral team and will include your website in the email, as well.'

"If the response to your conversation is positive, just follow what I have told you, but if they tell you that they are not interested for whatever reason, then don't try to sell them. Your purpose is only to invite them to the meeting. You are not there to peddle your group to them.

"The group will persuade guests to apply, or it will eliminate itself from consideration. You are only inviting to expose the person to your group. Before I tell you how to respond to someone being negative toward your invitation, I want to tell you that there are three reasons why people will want to apply for membership to your group."

1. Energy – If your members have no energy and guests would rather attend a funeral than visit your group a second time, they will not want to be part of it. If your group has great energy, they will want to be there. Although there are four basic temperaments of people and each temperament enjoys differing environments, no one enjoys a lifeless entourage of business professionals.
2. Welcome – People want to feel genuinely welcomed when they attend a meeting. I often tell members of the chapters that I manage that when we have guests

don't feel like your conversation with another member is so important that you overlook a guest.

"When Tim attends a networking function and the meeting has adjourned, he has a habit of standing by the back door and shaking everyone's hand. Guests will normally arrive early and leave early. When Tim stands at the back door, he is able to converse with each guest which goes a long way towards making him or her feel welcome."

"Cathy, now that you mention it, I noticed when I met him at the Chamber meeting a week ago today that he shook hands with and talked with everyone. There must have been 100 or so people there including the guests, members and staff members. It seems like everyone knew him."

"Clark, he never meets a strange, and probably most of those people did know him," stated Cathy.

3. Positive Revenue Numbers – If a group has 25 members, and they announce their revenue for the year as $25,000, that's only an average of $1000 per member. Those numbers would tell me that they are more of a social club. You will build lifelong relationships through networking and look forward to interacting with the members, but at the end of the day you will lose your desire to keep participating if they are not generating positive revenue. On the other hand, if a group has 25 members who have generated $500,000 worth of revenue, those numbers look so much better. Now we are talking about the average seat value of $20,000."

"Do you need anything else to drink?" asked the waitress.

Clark asked for some Mr. Pibb, and Cathy wanted more coffee.

"I apologize for taking that detour down a dirt road, but I had to make that clear. Let's get back to a negative response when you give the verbal invitation. There are a couple of different schools of thought on this.

1. Overflow – When Joseph the plumber says, 'I am way too busy to attend a meeting; I have all the business I need; I'm really not interested;' or any number of other responses, then simply ask, 'Where do you send your overflow business?' Joseph may say 'What overflow business?' You respond by saying, 'When a potential customer calls and he or she needs your service now, but you can't get there for two weeks.' If he really is too busy or doesn't have the time, he will give you the name of another plumber to whom he refers his overflow business. Then you go through the same process of inviting this new plumber.

2. Competition – Another way to deal with Joseph's negative response is when he says, 'I am way too busy to attend a meeting' or any number of other responses, then simply ask, 'Who is your biggest competitor, because my referral partners are looking to refer business to a plumber like you.' At this point in the conversation, he will usually do one of two things. He will rethink his answer because Joseph really does not want to lose out on the referrals, or if he really is too busy, he will give you the name of another plumber."

After pausing for a minute to drink some coffee, Cathy continued.

"Let's discuss inviting via mail and email.

"I will give this to you. I put this on my letterhead and wrote the letter to you. Remember this works with regular mail or email.

Hello, Clark,

I hope that this letter finds you well. The purpose for writing you is to tell you about a meeting I have with a group of business partners at 8:30 a.m. on Wednesdays at the 1818 Club on Sugarloaf Parkway. They are looking to refer pest control business to someone like you. I look forward to introducing you to my referral team. Bring plenty of business cards.

Sincerely,
Cathy Barbieri

"What would it mean to your business if you had five confirmed guests for each networking event that you attended? It would be huge. Regardless of what type of networking group you belong to, it would definitely set you apart from others. It has to become a mindset. Many times people become too focused on what is going on around them and too focused on working in their business instead of working on their business. By constantly inviting people, you will actually be working on your business. It gives you more people to whom you can refer business and from whom you can receive referred business.

"We spoke about focused inviting for your group and constantly inviting. Now, let's discuss inviting for the spotlight presenter. Most every week the group will have a member give a 7-10 minute presentation. A brilliant idea is to find out who the speaker would like to have in the room to hear him or her speak, and then invite several people that work in that industry.

"Let me give you an example. The Mortgage Broker tells the group he would like to have Realtors in the room. If you are in a closed networking group, you will have only one Realtor, but in other groups there may be several Realtors. The main purpose for inviting the other Realtors is to expose them to the Mortgage Broker. They are exposed to the entire chapter, but that happens as a byproduct.

"Earlier, we discussed several ways to find a particular classification. Once you have received the name of several Realtors and as much contact information as possible, the best way to contact him or her is face to face or via the telephone.

"The conversation would go something like this:

'Hello, John, I am Cathy. The purpose of contacting you is to let you know that Jeff Rack, a fabulous Mortgage Broker, is going to be speaking at a meeting this Wednesday at the 1818 Club on Sugarloaf at 8:30 a.m. Do you have a relationship with a Mortgage Broker?'

"If John answers, 'Yes' tell him that maybe after hearing Jeff speak he could use Jeff as a backup. If he answers 'No' then say, 'I'd love to introduce you to him. He is one of the best in the area.'

"I gave you several scripts to use for inviting someone to your business meeting. Now let me tell you what works for me. I tell people my story."

Example of conversation:

'Joseph, how are you doing today?'

'Fine.'

'Have you seen the kind of growth in your business that you'd like to see, and are you reaching your financial goals?'

'I could always use more customers, and I'd like to do better at reaching my goals.'

'Let me tell you one thing that has worked for our company. We had not been in business very long when Tim invited me to a networking meeting. At first, I thought it was some kind of gimmick until he explained the concept. I went to the meeting and when I saw the amount of referrals being passed, I applied for membership to the group. It has been the best business decision we have ever made. Last year alone 72 percent of our business came through this avenue. I think it would be great for your business.'

"By simply telling my story, people will at least show up to see if it could work for them.

"Tim should be here soon so I will leave you with one last bit of information to consider. You should spend four to six hours per week networking. Time will be spent at the meeting, looking for referrals for your partners, having one-to-ones and inviting guests to grow your network. Don't ever think that you are a champion networker because you show up for a meeting every week. You must work on it daily."

Just as she finished, Tim walked into Curt's.

"Cathy, were you able to finish?" asked Tim.

"Yes. Your timing could not have been better."

"While I was out, I spoke with the owner of a local property management firm about carpet cleaning. He said they have been using a company that gives them a cheap price but often when they finish cleaning the carpet, the carpet is still dirty. I gave him one of your cards, and explained how thorough your technicians are. He said he would call this afternoon, but he wanted me to give you his card in case he got busy and didn't make the call. He said to call him tomorrow after 10:00 a.m., if he doesn't call today."

"Thanks, Tim. I really appreciate that."

"I appreciate you taking time to educate Clark," Tim replied. "From all indications, he will be a networking guru."

"I have to run, but I will see you in a couple of months."

"Sounds good," answered Tim.

"Cathy taught you the last piece of networking," Tim stated. "If you apply all of the information that the different educators have taught you, you will have stunning results."

"Where do I start?" asked Clark.

"How are you set financially?"

"My wife makes a decent salary, but the pest control business has not taken off yet."

"Would you be able to swing $1000-$1500 right now?"

"I really can't swing that much, but I have a company credit card."

"Visit the closed networking groups in the area, and when you find the one that best suits you, fill out an application," said Tim. "Join the Chamber of Commerce, too. Then apply everything that you have learned.

"If you join these groups and follow the system for a full year, it will be one of best business decisions that you have ever made. If you don't feel like it was a good decision, I will personally refund your money. I think you will be surprised at the results. Every year it gets better and better."

"That's what I'll do," replied Clark. "Monday I will join the Chamber of Commerce. When do the closed networking groups meet?"

"Some chapters meet on Tuesday, some on Wednesday and others on Thursday. The time varies from group to group. Some groups meet as early as 7:00 a.m., but others meet for lunch."

"Tim, I can't thank you enough for everything. I've learned so much about how networking really operates, and each and every person who helped me was incredible. Now how much do I owe you? Do you take credit cards?"

"Clark, I told you it would be affordable," declared Tim. "The cost is that you must learn the system well, have it become so much a part of you that it is second nature, and then you must help others learn to become champion networkers. We want to change the way our community does business."

"That's all?" asked Clark incredulously. "What I have learned is easily worth $5,000, but you don't want any money. Are you for real, or are you jerking my chain?"

"I'm for real," answered Tim. "Since you will be joining the Chamber, I will be able to monitor your progress at the meetings. Perhaps I'll see you at your closed networking group, as well."

CHAPTER 9

Six Months Later

On Friday, after a fantastic Chamber meeting, Tim and Clark met for lunch at the Philly Connection to discuss his development.

After they placed their order, they sat down to talk.

"Clark, I want you to know that I am proud of the progress you have made. Your infomercials have been on target. You have hit all of the key components every time that I have heard you. You have always given us your name, company name, focused on only one aspect of what you do, given facts or told a short story that supports your LCD, ask for a specific referral and finished with your name and company name. I applaud you for this. You have stayed the course and have not deviated."

"Thanks, Tim. That means more to me than you realize."

"Clark, do you feel as if you made a wise decision joining the Chamber and a closed networking group?"

"Well, I'll put it this way; you will not have to refund my money. It was slow for the first three months, but then we started to gain some traction. It has been wonderful. As a matter of fact, probably in the next three to four months, I'll look to join a service-oriented group."

"Awesome! Two weeks ago when you gave your 7-minute presentation, I noticed that you educated the group on two LCD's, told stories related to those LCD's and then told us how to refer you related to those LCD's. I also noted that when they asked if anyone had questions, you only called on two people, although 15 different people raised their hand."

"That's correct. David Alexander taught me to plant questions. I planted three questions, but I only had time to answer two of them."

"Excellent," replied Tim. "For the past three months, when the ambassador who facilitates the meeting asks for the number of referrals that were passed since last week's meeting, you have always passed at least one. One week, I observed that you had passed five referrals."

"Again, Tim, you are correct. I want to be a networking guru just like you. If I could learn to be another Jamie Harrelson from North Carolina, it would make my day. She is the referral Wonder Woman."

Tim responded with, "That she is, that she is. She is so incredible that it seems as if she is a fairy tale."

After D.P. Patel brought their Philly sandwiches with extra cheese and peppercorn to the table, they began to eat. After finishing their sandwiches, they continued their conversation.

"Clark, have you found time to meet with other members outside of the scheduled meetings?"

"I have. I schedule at least 1 one-to-one every week. Occasionally, I am able to schedule two in a week. It has been beneficial to learn more about the members than what I can learn from only hearing their infomercials or presentations. In this area, I don't know if I'll ever measure up to what you did, but it's at least a start."

"Clark, if you will maintain at least one per week, you'll marvel at how well you will be able to refer to other members. Other members will be able to refer to you as well."

"Since I have experienced this first hand, I whole heartedly agree."

"Have you had the opportunity to give kudos to other members?"

"A little bit, but not nearly as much as maybe I should. The infomercials, presentation skills, passing referrals and scheduling one-to-ones have come a little easier than giving testimonials about others. Probably as I practice more, I will be able to improve in this area."

"I agree," Tim replied.

"One other area that I don't quite have down is inviting people to the meeting. I use the G.R.I.P method that Cathy taught me, but so far in six months only 20 guests have shown up that I have personally invited. I know that's low, and I need to work on it."

"Clark, in truth, that shocks me. If a member brings one guest per month, they are doing an admirable job of inviting."

"Wow! That makes me feel a little bit better. I think I somehow thought I need to pass one referral per week, have one guest per week and schedule one one-to-one per week."

"Clark, if you maintain that ideology, you will definitely become a champion networker.

"I have another appointment in a few minutes, but I want to leave you with this. Your progression astounds me. You have been working at this for six months. I want you to give it one full year. When you have learned each system well enough that you can teach it to others, let's sit down again and discuss the results. At that time, I would also like to introduce you to some more of my friends who will teach you concepts that will take your business to the next level."

SPECIAL THANKS

Special thanks to all of the people who have assisted with this book. When we began this venture, I had no idea this project would take as long as it did, or that this book would have to be edited so much.

Cindi Dowdle with Atlanta AdGraphics once again impressed me with her work. Many times over the past several years, I have described what I needed designed, and she has always created the exact picture. The cover of this book displays her unbelievable talent.

Many people participated in the editing of this book.

Melanie Morgan with Maverick Marketing Design took a very rough draft that had little punctuation and gave me back a workable project.

My wife, Brenda Barber, has read through the book at least 20 times to check for mistakes; she has also been my sounding board for various ideas and concepts.

Kathy Copeland was my go-to editor. I called or texted her several times to ask her grammatical questions.

Art Kleve, David Alexander, David Lawler, Gina Herald, Derek Sutton and Cathy Barbieri gave me much-needed feedback.

When I thought we had a perfect manuscript, my friend, David Alexander, recommended sending it to Elizabeth Paulin for the final edit. When I spoke with her, I explained that the book probably wouldn't need much editing. One week after I sent her the manuscript, she sent it back with several corrections that needed to be made. Thanks, David, for the advice and thanks, Elizabeth, for the editing.

I was humbled that when Bob Burg sent me his endorsement, he also sent several suggestions for changes that would make the book better. Since his incredible books have helped many, I heeded his advice.

My cousin and everyone's favorite, Theresa O'Kelley spent several hours on the final edit. Words can't describe my appreciation for the contributions she made to this book.

James Barber is married to Brenda, and they have two daughters, two sons-in-law and three grandchildren.

They currently own Training of Champions and ICN Publications. James is a BNI director consultant, a volunteer ambassador with the Gwinnett County Chamber of Commerce, one of the largest and most active Chambers in the United States. He proudly served in the Navy. He and his company have won numerous awards. He is a coach, trainer, motivational speaker and author. He loves people, and is very passionate about helping small business owners. He desires for this book to be a blessing to all who read it.

Book 2 of *The Networking Guru* series, *The Next Level*, should be published by Jan 2016. To schedule James to speak at your event or for corporate training, contact him at 770-287-3131 or www.thenetworking-guru.com.

CPSIA information can be obtained at www.ICGtesting.com
Printed in the USA
LVOW11s2014220815

451170LV00003B/5/P